WINTER
EVOCATIONS

Published by Sophie Kilic
© Sophie Kilic 2021

ISBN 978-1-78222-823-3

Book design, layout and production management
by Into Print
www.intoprint.net
+44 (0)1604 832149

WINTER
EVOCATIONS

To my amazing family and friends.
Thank you all.

INTRODUCTION

Winter is the season which many people dread. The rounds of coughs and colds, the cold, the wet, the long dark nights. Everything seems to require more effort and many of us would like either to hibernate or migrate to the other side of the world. Yet the understated English winter can be a season full of hope, wonder and joy. This is a book to hopefully lift the spirits, something to dip into and savour over a comforting hot drink, to help us connect with the winter and the many marvels which it holds.

MORNINGS

Dawn

The sky was creeping into a voluminous clarity as I set off this morning. Yet at dawn's first tint, when an inky blue breath subtly stole through the shadows and I stayed snuggled under a duvet, birdsong was already bright, drawing me into a new day. The crisp clarity of a frosty morning always coaxes me out; energised by its cutting edge; each grass blade beautifully embellished as a cake with sugar crystals, every oak leaf sporting a sparkling rim and each berry a bead of glittering marcasite. The birch trees looked graceful this morning. Stripped of all attire, they revealed a fragility which trembled in the breaking blue blush of dawn. Frost feathers adorned windscreens; small miracles of form catching the light of the sun like cut glass. There is so much wonder in winter, so much beauty to behold.

It is during winter that we perhaps feel closer to nature and the part we play in it, for we see it as it is, unadulterated in the stark landscapes and skeletal trees. We feel its fresh clarity on sunny days and under starry skies and identify with its vulnerability, the fact that like us it faces death. On other days nature is powerful, the strength of a storm compelling, when the wind stirs a surge of excitement from deep within. Oak leaves, also stirred up, fly through the air, following the playful patterns of skittish circular pathways like excited children and dogs. There are so many circles stimulating different responses: the circle of seasons and time, hands on a clock moving imperceptibly around its face, ticking towards winter, or counting down to midnight. There is the motion of stirring Christmas pudding wishes, or the deep chocolate comfort of cocoa turned slowly with a spoon. Circles are created when a cat curls up or a restless dog turns around and around until, exhausted, he finally sinks down in front of the fire and sleeps.

Geese

Before the moon melted into the blue dream of day, sunrise had unfurled its flaming fingers to awaken trees, which seemed to stretch their limbs in a world where nothing stirred. Suddenly, above my head, migrating geese, bellies bronzed, formed a gilded arrow as they soared through the silent sky with apparent ease on a journey that could cost them everything. We can learn from such instinctive trust, co-operation, hope and strength to persevere; for without this faith we fall. On that radiant morning, I witnessed the miracle of bird migration, one of life's many miracles which we take so for granted, including, of course, the miracle of life itself.

Dawn wanderings

In the calm blue serenity of dawn light I crunch through frost-crisped leaves which sparkle in the streetlights. I have stepped from my front door into a world waiting, a wonderland laid out beneath the stretching shadows of skeletal trees. All frost-fingered surfaces sparkle; each adorned and decorated. The most flat-faced featureless fence has been transformed and tangles of brown thicket have adopted a new dimension. In the ice blue-grey of early morning these sparkling surfaces reflect the facets of a robin's metallic melody; the sound of burnished steel chiselled by a blackbird's anvilling alarm call.

As I walk, twigs snap and crack under-foot with a brittle-ice fragility and puddles shatter, puddles which, when looked into, reveal patterns like a piece of abstract art. Wrens tick me off at the disturbance while cold freezes fingers and pinches cheeks. Yet this is the best time to be about, to appreciate the surreal stillness of this winter world which waits for those who take notice. And in its beautiful dream, I walk, exhilarated. With each step, the sky lifts a little, a creeping blush of sunlight seeping into the brightening dome so that the moon, set at its centre, softly fades. And above the dark forms of skeletal trees, a mini murmuration of early birds rides through the saffron sunlight spill which stretches from the horizon and hovers above the blank canvas of the frosted fields; fields spread as with a white sheet, slightly grey in the nacreous half-light. This is a new world waiting, revealing its whis-pered wonders like an open book, its pris-tine pages unmarred by man, drawing me into their anticipation and the excitement which stirs with the opening chapter of a new day.

This Morning

This morning
A robin's sharp, silver-edged song
Sliced my subconscious
Dividing dreams
From the waking world
So that my eyes opened.

It dawned on me then,
Slowly, that it was still night
And this song,
So bright in its diamond-hard brilliance
Juxtaposed darkness
Like anomalies in dreams.

Swimming in a state
Somewhere above
The subconscious
I went out,
Compelled by the chorus.
I stood on the cusp of dawn,
Its spiky frost formations
And glittering surfaces
Reflecting the crisp clarity
Of the robin's notes.

And wandering under the last lingering stars
Which pierced the lifting canopy of night,
Everything made sense suddenly
And I held in my heart
The same exuberance
As the robin
Who sat in the shadows
And sang.

Watermeadows

A white world of mist and hoar frost. The sun rises, cutting through the contrails of the clouds with its amber orb. A nacreous sky melds with the mist which rises gently from the ground and hovers in curls above the river like a horse's steaming breath. Skeletal trees take on subtle forms, subdued to grey ghosts, intricate and beautiful in the pearly light. History haunts these water meadows for these trees are ancient and the river has taken these twists and turns since centuries began. Even the farmhouse; its three chimneys black against the glowing sky, has perhaps been here a hundred years or more, gently humanising this timeless scene of stunning beauty; so stunning that I wish I had my camera to capture it in photos as well as words.

Coast

Sunshine spills onto the shingle as it rises on a new winter morning. In the still, reflective calm, nobody is about, just gulls which wander about the tideline looking for food or sit, looking on at the crashing waves. The sea inhales and exhales deeply, as if revelling in the fresh clarity of morning air and atmosphere, a clarity so crisp that coats, hats and gloves are needed. There is a depth which cannot be fathomed, something so immense that I feel absorbed by it, lost in its intensity. Sunlight is sifted as heavy clouds muscle in, trying to usurp it. Its apocalyptic rays reach down through these clouds to spangle the sea. The sun's appearance might be fleeting but it has brought joy to the morning and even though it might disappear from view, it will still be there as a beacon of hope behind the winter clouds, a hope which warms our hearts. *(Abbotsbury)*

Antiquity

As the morning light lifts, the sun sieving wan rays of light through ashen shreds of cloud, a pair of swans glide with nonchalance along the river. Stillness; nobody about, the only sounds being the occasional river splash, the tick of a wren from a nearby bush. Before the river stands an ancient oak, centuries old. Lightly frosted leaf litter still lies about its base, its bark rough and chill to the touch. It is sleeping now. Sleeping through another season of another century as it has done for hundreds of years. There is a beauty to behold in its gnarled and knotted limbs, the whorls and waves in the wood creating mesmerising patterns. It gives life to a host of insects and plants, an entire ecosystem. I climb inside the hollow trunk to be closer to its interior, its mellow heart, for I feel that if it could talk, it would have tales to tell. Looking up into its crown, I am insignificant as it towers above. This is the king of trees, the oak. Oaks have been used as hiding places for real kings. In 1651 King Charles II hid inside an oak in Boscobel wood, Shropshire, in order to successfully escape the Roundheads. This became known as "The Royal Oak" and although the original tree doesn't survive, it is still the name of many pubs around the country today.

Those days of civil war were truly days of uncertainty and there have been many more since. This tree, inside which I now sit, would have been alive during those days, with the same river running past. The little church with the square tower which I see across the water meadows would have also been here. They have all been witness to bad times and to good, perhaps all have been safe havens, and all have certainly survived the test of time. Although time changes and times change, certain things remain the same, both tangible and intangible, and when days become dark and uncertain, it is the permanent and unchanging which provide a sense of security and respite. *(Dorset Stour)*

Tawny owl

A sickle moon cut into the half-light this morning, slicing the sky with its needle thin brilliance. It was accompanied by Venus which hung motionless beside it; remote and icy, another faraway world, which we cannot quite fathom, looking down aloof into our own from its lofty heights. And at half past six, still dark, a tawny started to hoot; sitting in an oak just above where I stood, that vagrant, ethereal call which sends quivers through the hearts of rodents and sends a delicious slither of excitement and mystery through my own. So the soft sound of the tawny drew in the dawn, slices of sound reverberating off the suspended chill. I stood and listened, captivated by nature's small wonders; the silent stars, the moon, and the proximity of the tawny owl unperturbed by my presence as I passed.

Ice wonders

The tentative trickle of a blackbird's fluid note seeps into the dawn like the first light stealing into the sky. The walk to the bus stop takes me along twinkling pathways; a million minute stars sparkling beneath my feet, on fences and garden walls, stars surrounding me where the frost has fallen. The way is slippery, slow, yet the air resonates with the robins' jingling choruses, coming from all quarters on the cold breath of twilight. The moon, still strong, bright and full, hangs in a sky which is drawing into day and as light lifts into its immense canopy, so trees stand silhouetted against an intense blue backlight. Brown bracken fronds are beautified in their crystalline cloaks like sugar coating on a cake, a sparkling crust revealing the intricate structure of each pinnae. But it is the bus-stop roof which takes my breath away, the glass roof where perfect frost formations flow and fuse like wallpaper patterns. These are the "frost-ferns" I've always heard about – but to me, thinking of the bracken behind me, I think of them more as frost feathers gently sweeping, brushing; each "frond" overlapping. Such wonder in this natural formation, an etching in ice as if it were manmade. Once the day is up and risen, clad in pink, white, and sparkly silver, the ice will melt away, stolen by the sun and the crisp clarity of a winter's day.

More ice wonders

As the first flush of daylight seeps into the sky, merging with monochrome, I am drawn into more dimensions, surrounded by the sound of blackbirds clipping the cold air with their morning calls. Frost formations on glass resemble a chaotic display of individual orb-webs, each "web" about three centimetres in diameter, spun with warp and weft and messily joined to another with a tangle of more warp threads so that angles collide in criss-crossed lines. Every icy "thread" seems to be embroidered, embellished by a crystalline inflorescence, astounding in its fernlike intricacy, compounding a wonderful sense of mystery, for in the past, the legendary Jack Frost fascinated people with his secret bursts of nocturnal creativity. My sense of wonder is brought on by the beauty of what can be created naturally, still remaining mysterious, even though science has an explanation for it. It is my own secret spectacle with no one to share it at such an early hour. Never having my camera on such unexpectedly exquisite moments on the way to work, I will have to be satisfied with the joy of exclusive discovery and of keeping the image eternally etched on my memory, for once they warm, these intricate ice patterns melt away and are lost forever.

Museum

On a bright sunny morning during the Christmas holidays I decide to visit a local museum. I leave the house, walking past frost-blanched rooftops and verges, which glow golden pink in the rising sunlight. The museum, set in a 16th century house, provides an intimate record of local history. I step across crooked floors, embraced by the smell of wood and beeswax which rise to greet me. The house has been decorated for Christmas, to show how it would have been celebrated during different centuries and in the entrance hall, a tall Christmas tree covered in ribbons and candles ushers in Victorian times. It was Prince Albert who brought the tradition back from

Germany, and although some say that it is pagan, I think there is nothing wrong with bringing a bit of life into the home to lighten the mood of the season and to create a cosy atmosphere, my sense of aesthetic always being satisfied by a beautifully and tastefully decorated tree.

As I step through a small door with bent frame, I am stepping back in time, for in the parlour sit a model woman and man, she in a fitted black dress, her head covered in a white cap, he in a jacket and knee length boots. Their table, modest yet sumptuous, is covered with a starched white linen cloth, draped with greenery and set with simple white china, glass and silver. Functionality always seemed to be second to aesthetic then; everything elegant, including the serving dishes. On the sideboard stands a heavy meat pie and a bowl of fruit, both of which would have been a luxury in those days. Judging from the pale green panelled walls and the family portraits, I assume that this is a scene from the 18th century and that these people were comfortably off but not able to afford the excess and the extravagant luxury which would be found in the English country house. The scene evokes a sense of respectability, in that people would buy what they could afford for the festive season, however small. And whatever they had, they appreciated, preparing it well, maintaining high standards. Everything seems clean and well-presented. It reminds me of my grandmother's attitude, for however frugal times could be, she always provided the best.

The kitchen with its flagstone floor intrigues me most. This is where the food would have been prepared, the heart of the home with its fireside warmth and waft of comforting aromas. A huge dresser full of blue and white china stands beside a large stove, brass pots and pans hang on stone walls, the ceiling candelabras swathed in ivy. On a wooden table sit a pestle and mortar, a grater and a huge mixing bowl. I imagine the pudding, seasoned with spice, being stirred round and around while wishes were made so long ago. That again was a Victorian tradition and two puddings were often made; one for Christmas day and one for new year, into the centre of the latter a dried bean, a small thimble or penny placed for someone to find. The hiding of the bean inside a comestible goes back to at least Tudor times when it would have been placed within a twelfth night "cake" (an enriched fruited bread) . The Tudors celebrated the twelve days of Christmas culminating on twelfth night with much revelry, feasting and wassailing. The person who found the bean in his or her piece of cake would become the King or Queen of misrule for the night, being in charge of antics and entertainment, a tradition coming from the Roman winter festival of Saturnalia.

I wander through more rooms comprising the many displays of artefacts and memorabilia, and teaching me much about the lives of ordinary people. A small school room has been recreated; rows of simple single desks with wooden tops and ink wells set into the back. The village children would have tramped through fields to get here, come rain or shine and in the bitter winter cold.

Up the creaky stairs I climb, to rooms which would have once been bedrooms with uneven floors and small windows with wiggly glass through which you squint to see the street below. At this early hour the museum is so quiet, I feel as if I were standing in someone's house, reliving their dreams, their many memories. It is as if the clock were ticking imperceptibly through time, yet something were holding it all together like a continuous thread, a sense of experience which has not broken through the centuries.

Back downstairs I pass over more stone floors, smoothed by the many feet which have walked over and across them. I exit into the garden; small and still, it shivers in the cold. Frost fingers all, embellishing, beautifying, crystallising the earth. Flowerbeds lie fallow, lawns and small topiary hedges clipped into spheres are iced, an orb web gently trembles, catching the sunlight on its silken strands. There is nobody about. The house looks on, watching through blank windows, windows which have seen the centuries pass. It seems to watch while a fluffed-up blackbird picks through leaf litter and pecks at a flowerbed's frozen soil. Apart from nature going about its business, all is so still, the breeze in the bushes like a rustle of silk skirts, the air softly sculpted by a pigeon's croon, smoothing contours where sun and frost mingle. And so melting into one, the frost fades and the garden takes on a new day, one of dazzling sunshine and crisp cold. People appear at the doorway to take a stroll, memories melting as life slowly returns. (*Wimborne, Dorset*)

Intrusion

Early one morning we take a woodland walk. A pristine peaceful wonderland stretches before us through the trees, hushed and still as snow floats down, layer upon layer. Birds have ceased singing, the only sound of their presence a flick or a rustle as they desperately pick for food in bushes and scrub. So quiet is it, that only the gentle trickle of a stream coursing through the forest can be discerned, along with the almost imaginary flick of flakes on leaves as if the snow were audible; thick, velvety, falling like feathers through a sickly sky.

It feels as if we are the first to be about but are also being watched. I peer into the recesses between the trees, a cavernous white, echoing stillness. Nothing trembles nor stirs. And then we see tracks in the snow, wandering tracks, into the trees and then out again, looping and backing on themselves along the path. And there are not only one set of tracks. The imagination runs wild in a winter forest and one considers hobbits, trolls or even wolves, for the forest has become a fairy tale, a legendary white world where cold clamours against ears, ringing into the resounding silence like an imaginary gong and anything could happen. We jump at the slightest snap, the brush of a twig, a drop suspended, twinkling in the sunlight, suddenly falling. There are drops everywhere, resplendent as stars, natural decorations in a white world as if the forest had been prepared for something special. The trees cast soft shadows across the snow, shadows which stretch with the rising sun. We think the footsteps in the snow are possibly deer tracks, and that the animals, wishing to remain unseen, have escaped deeper into the tangle of thicket from where they can secretly observe us.

Nothing stays secret in snow, unless a layer comes to cover over, create a clean slate. The winter world reveals all. Yet these nocturnal perambulations give us a sense of shared space, a sense of the many unseen creatures which remain secretly here, and that despite the silence and the apparent lack of life, wildlife is abundant, choosing, with its instinctive fear of man, to live apart from us. It is sad that as humans we have caused nature to become so afraid. Our past record of hunting and exploitation of the natural world has only made us its enemies and I feel for the first time as if I am trespassing on a perfect world, that my crunching footsteps sully the snow and that we have no right to be here.

Sunday morning

The sun had been up for about an hour when I went out into the chill of a clear morning. It was minus seven last night and everything seemed fresh, vibrant, crystal cut. The house sparrows in the back garden were already about their business, flitting to and fro from the camellia bush to the eaves of the house, chirruping constantly. Frost on the fence top steamed, sending up languid, curling trails; a breath so easily expelled in the morning sun. Outside the front, the air stayed serene and calm, echoing with the croon of woodpigeons, a soothing serenade warming the chill. Deep golden light hung in the tree canopies, sunshine suspended. A starling whistled, a pigeon clapped its wings, bushes sparkled in the sun's rays as they obliquely caught flecks of frost. It was as if each bare branch had been adorned with tiny twinkling stars. I passed shattered puddles, where children had stamped; every puddle a puzzle, whose fractured face was hard to piece together. We like to deface, destroy... it is the same with pristine snow, which soon looks sullied once people have played in it. But that morning, despite the puddles, everything bore beauty, displaying in its simplicity something remarkable, and for that moment held suspended in sunlight, the day held its breath in optimism, anticipation and joy.

Wet weekend

It is a delicious state when waking with the slow realisation that you do not have to get up for work. This realisation seeps in gradually, sinking into the soft recesses of the pillow and cushioning you with an ecstasy of comfort. This is especially so in the winter when cold dark mornings, often wet and windy, are not conducive to getting up and going outside. Eager to return to the twilight land of shallow sleep, to harness unfinished dreams, after which the awakening will be into the real world, a world of daylight rather than one which is dark, I snuggle down beneath the duvet. And as the wind exhales deeply, cavorting with the trees, whipping their branches into a delirious frenzy, and rain peppers the window with stinging drops, I feel fortunate to be in a warm bed and to be able to continue in that carefree dream world of restorative sleep.

A Christmas carol

Early on Christmas morning
Before the dawn
Flushed its amber hue
Across the vast swathe of sky
The morning star
Rang out;
A bell in a pellucid eternity.
And it was as if all the stars were singing
The medieval harmony of the celestial
spheres,
Rejoicing that the day had come
To commemorate
The birth of one
So long ago
Who yet birthed them
When time was born.

MEMORY AND IMAGINATION

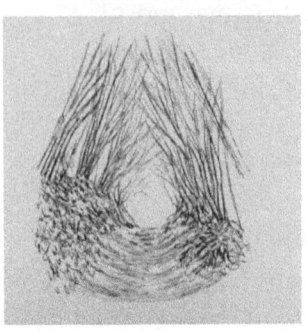

Ship of the Fen

As a child I was captivated by the Ship of the Fens, as she sailed the horizon, an elusive phantom, appearing and disappearing in and out of the fog which hovered over flat fields. She was a lady in grey, enigmatic, mysterious and compellingly beautiful, bearing a serenity on those bleak grey fenland days when the wind scoured across the flats, searing cold. I had read that in the 19th century, it was possible to skate along the river into Ely, the ice was so thick. I had read that the skaters marvelled at the cathedral architecture with its strong stone facades which had weathered the winters of centuries, standing as a focal point within the small city and outside it on the empty horizon.

Cathedrals are particularly poignant at Christmas with their floodlit exteriors, glowing candlelit interiors and uplifting carol services. Floodlights emphasise the architecture, the wonders of symmetry and design and the great skill and craftsmanship which our predecessors exhibited in the execution of these fantastic works; expressions of their love, faith and dedication. Ely is no exception with the smooth contours of its tower softly bathed in light and the octagon picked out in a brighter floodlight. Yet this rather unsubtle enhancement of the octagon from the outside is nothing compared to its sight from within, for it is a wonder which draws your eyes forever upwards so that you cannot stop looking, staring with a child's captivation.

The Fens look particularly forlorn in winter. Old houses meld into the mist, market towns often seem sleepy, or they did to me as a child. The area is steeped in history; a land salvaged from the sea, a wetland drained. Must Farm, a Bronze Age settlement discovered near Whittlesey, reveals the sophisticated lifestyle of the inhabitants. Their circular houses, built on stilts above a river around 3,000 years ago, were a hub of activity. People wove fine fabric from plant fibres, made domestic objects of metal and wood, wore beads and jewellery and used a variety of ceramic pots. I imagine them crouching by the fire which burned within the middle of their circular abodes. It must have been cold and damp and the fire would have warmed them and even kept them alive during the winter months. Was it perhaps one of these fires which got out of control and sent sparks spreading to other dwellings, or was it arson? Whatever happened, the houses burnt, falling into the river. The fire was instantly extinguished, the houses buried in silt and mud which preserved them and everything else. It is thought that a similar fire destroyed prehistoric huts on stilts at nearby Flag Fen, causing them also to fall into the water and remain in situ under the silt. These are bleak tales as bleak as a fenland winter day, of lives being extinguished like a candle in a breath of wind. And yet their legacy lives on, and from it we gain a deeper understanding of the past from what was left behind.

Tales of Christmas past

Up in the attic an Alladin's cave awaited us. I was a teenager in an emporium full of treasures which held many memories. We entered the loft from the attic space through a small door, ducking our heads and poking around in the lowlight labyrinth of boxes, bags, tuckboxes and trunks. I pulled out a box; dusty cardboard which tickled the back of my nose and throat, and dragged it down the spiral stairs, precariously. It bounced and bumped. I could have carried it actually, for it was quite light. One of the trunks was much heavier, made of metal with sharp corners. That would have to stay in situ, along with all the other bric-a-brac and memorabilia of an entire life, yet I couldn't resist lifting the lid. I was greeted with an aroma of dust and damp, an array of fabrics oddly assorted. This was the dressing up box of childhood. I peeped at clothes from nativity plays; an angel in white with a glittering halo, and a sheep. That costume had been so hot, made of wool blanket by my mother. I had prickled and itched but it had looked the part as I followed the shepherds around the stage. Next some of the cocktail dresses my great aunts wore for going out in the 1920s; slender and trim, made of heavy, scratchy synthetic, which glittered when they walked. It was considered a novelty then. I imagined the parties, socialising away the winter after work, or maybe they were ladies of leisure in those days. I remembered trying these dresses on, swamped. Yet they had felt glamourous with my mother's old high heels; the excitement of putting on a new persona was creative and fun back then. Now we perhaps do it all the time, unconsciously, depending on who we are trying to talk to.

The trunk had taken my attention but it was the box I wanted. And there it was at the bottom of the stairs. Kneeling on the floor, I ripped off the previous year's brown tape and delved inside. A treasure trove of decorations awaited, each that I held in my hand telling a story.

I have the same box before me today and now I delve in deeply. Here are the German decorations, paper-frail yet wooden; stars and snowflakes sent by a friend. The straw stars were made by my uncle, lots of them; an entire galaxy waiting to be hung. Delving deeper I find the decorations which I loved as a child, always putting them in pride of place at the front of the tree; next come the old glass baubles, all individually wrapped in their crinkled, foxed tissue. These have hung on our trees forever, twinkling with reflected fairy lights, drawing a sense of captivation and excitement.

Every part of rediscovering decorations is enjoyable. It is like eating layers of a hugely tiered delicious cake one by one and savouring each for itself. The anticipation of unwrapping, of seeing familiar faces and meeting old memories. Here are a set of tiny red felt stockings; one for each member of the family, made by grandmother. We will miss her and my grandad this year, as we miss them every year, for they were always with us. Christmas can be nostalgic, sometimes one of the saddest times when we remember those who are no longer here, those who we still love. The cake has become bitter sweet.

As a child, the highlight of the lead up to Christmas was decorating the tree. The resinous smell of pine, the prickle of needles up finger nails and on the backs of hands. After my dad had woven the lights around and between branches, I would place each piece carefully, covetously, feeling extremely frustrated if anyone hung an item in a place which, to my eyes, didn't aesthetically align. Yet it was not just the sense of satisfaction when everything looked lovely - the cosy magic when one turned on the lights and saw everything creatively set out on its stage coming to life; but it was the memories of love, the associations of each decoration with a person, and the anticipation of joys to come.

Decorations are merely frivolities, something to tickle the sense of aesthetic and allow creativity to flow. They might hold meaning and sentiment but they are peripheral to the real message of Christmas. However, they do remind us of family and friends, of laughter and love and I will perhaps start making them for others, for them to take out each year, and remember something of me.

Decking the hall

Another wonder of the countdown to Christmas is decorating the house with greenery. When I was young, this was always my father's job. We would go together to snip trails of ivy which he would weave through the banisters and drape over the grandfather clock in the hall. We would come in from the garden, arms laden with holly, sometimes bright with berries but more often not. I would beg my mother to buy a sprig of mistletoe from the vegetable shop which we would hang in the porch to catch unsuspecting guests. As children we thought this was the height of amusement.

Banisters draped, each picture frame topped with a holly sprig, mistletoe hung and other installations of greenery accomplished, we wandered around the house in a state of exhilaration. For my father never decorated the house before Christmas Eve, as he wanted the greenery to last. Therefore we knew that this was a sign; the house was ready, carols would be playing, my mother would be baking in the kitchen so that aromas filled the air. I would assemble some apples in bowls, picked from the garden during the autumn, wrapped in newspaper and put in a dark shed. We all had to help.

We knew once all this was done, that the first of the family would soon be arriving for afternoon tea around the fire and then later the others for an evening meal so that by the time we went to bed on Christmas Eve, everyone would be together.

Old books

One winter weekend I went to Brighton to visit a friend. We spent the afternoon in the old part of town wandering tiny backstreets, perusing second hand bookshops, and sitting in small, overheated teashops consuming copious amounts of tea and cake while catching up. I came back on the train clutching a bag of several leather-bound books, each exciting and intriguing, each a story waiting to be discovered.

I love books, especially old ones. And on a winter's night years later I sit before the fire with one of these books waiting to rediscover its story. In fact its true story has never been discovered and I still wonder at its past. It was inscribed in the 18th century in looping copper plate by a British woman whose name remains a mystery in that she is neither famous nor even known. As the book is in French, she must have been educated, one of the wealthy who learned to speak French and perhaps Latin, as well as learning to draw, to play the piano and to sing; such were the expected accomplishments of young ladies of the day.

I imagine her in a big house, sitting in front of a fire as I do now, clocks ticking, the peaceful stillness of an elegant interior contrasting the creaking sigh of the wind outside. Through the heavily draped window perhaps lay a formal garden, grounds with large leafless trees stretching away to an obscure and dusky horizon, a horizon which would never be reached.

Her life would have been mapped out for her, her marriage fixed, her horizons set in the expectation of childbirth and being the lady of the home. With hours to kill, to please herself, she would have no doubt relished the company of the fireside, the escape into a book. For books take us out of ourselves and our situations and transport us to a different place. Story telling has always been part of community and culture, it helps bring people together, to explain and clarify, it helps us remember important truths and to share sentiments and experiences. Books commit these ideas, feelings and thoughts to paper as well as telling a story, the human story.

And so in some way I share only a fraction of her story, for all I know about her is that she owned the book which I hold in my hands 250 years later. I am its custodian through time until someone else holds it after I have gone. No one will know that I held it, yet her legacy lives in the signature inscribed on the first page. I know nothing of who owned it after her, who held it in their hands. Only she intrigues me.

So, curled up in the cosy glowing firelight, after pausing on the first page, I move on, turning the pages to read the words which she once read. French flows off the paper, transporting me to a different time and a different place away from this wintery world and into one of imagination and fantasy.

Winter sun

Lost in an evergreen forest. Strong winter sunshine filters through soldier straight ranks of conifer and pine, sending misty shafts to Midas touch brown bracken fronds. Out of the wind it is mild, gentle, the last of the oak leaves lingering copper, while delicate birch shines whiter than scintillated snow. A pigeon warmly croons and a robin's bright penny song spangles the silence. Wild fir trees like large Christmas trees are dwarfed by the immensity of space, a space slightly spiced by resin.

In the neighbouring countryside, cottages with smoke-curling chimneys bask in the brilliance of the day, their warm winter thatches keeping out the chill, small windows refusing to reveal the warm heart of the home. The air, wood smoked, tingles with the tattle of starlings, and the shriek of seagulls as they pass.

Out on the coast path the landscape rolls away in undulating sun-soaked coastline; ancient, full of fossils. Peace, permanent, but felt more strongly in winter, hangs like the low sun softly spreading across the looking glass surface of the sea, an antique looking glass, slightly mottled and foxed as small clouds sweep over, marbling the sky. Sheep with backlit golden fleece graze in sun flooded fields, greedily ripping at the turf with a guzzling munch. Dry teasels whisper and hiss in a brisk westerly while we walk with long shadows, rejuvenated by the sun and its bright winter optimism.

Winter rain

One wet winter's afternoon a friend and I decide to go for a drive. We take the car down single track country lanes, displacing puddles in the pot-holed road, wipers swishing frantically. Smeary windows distort dark trees, gaunt and stoic they stand soaked. A flustered pheasant makes a dash for it, diving head first into a twiggy hedgerow. Superstition stalks these Dartmoor lanes; the wild countryside has probably barely changed and is studded with prehistoric remnants. It is too wet for a walk so we stop in Drewsteignton. The picture postcard village comprising a pretty square, lined on both sides by old cottages which lead towards the church, looks dank and dejected. Nobody is about except for a couple of bedraggled hikers and a man in a deer stalker, wellies and a wax jacket pulling his reluctant retriever on a lead. Rain lashes down, making the cottages seem even cosier, their windows glowing. The man goes into one of them and closes the front door. The village holds a sense of refuge with its square of historic solidarity sheltering inhabitants from both the elements and the unrelenting moor beyond. The pub looks warm and welcoming but first we do some sightseeing, diving into the church having dashed from the car, holding hoods up against the chill wind and wet.

A contained atmosphere, something which I can't explain, grips us both so that we stand in silence. It is as if the church were a sanctuary away from the world, a heart beating inaudibly, a place of refuge flooding us with a feeling of security much stronger than the square. It is as if the years of centuries have stood still in this space and haven't moved. The outside world is remotely tangible, the muffled clatter of heavy rain ricocheting off gutters, the echoing patter on window and roof making us feel deliciously satisfied. It is that cosy under-canvas feeling, that survival instinct of finding somewhere dry to hunker down.

But it is more than that, the atmosphere keeps compelling as if embracing us, enveloping us within it.

On a scrap of paper left on a pew, somebody has scribbled, perhaps in desperate hope, "please pray for my son who is seriously ill." And then a quote, seemingly unrelated but perhaps written as if to point the person praying in the right direction, "Let us acknowledge the Lord; let us press on to acknowledge him. As surely as the sun rises, he will appear; he will come to us like the winter rains." Snug in this church on a petulant afternoon in winter, the rains have certainly come.

Scotland (near Loch Lomond)

Scotland experiences proper winters when to be huddled in a bothy beside a smoking fire, reading or writing equates with pure pleasure while the wind howls and rain lashes outside. For a southerner like me, these winters can be slightly overwhelming, for here we are at the mercy of the elements, but coming well-prepared, we take our chances in all weathers. A mountain hike one day leaves hearts in mouths as we struggle through spectacular scenery. The day is non-descript, brooding even; melancholy clouds lie low across the undulating, snow-speckled landscape which rises and falls in troughs and peaks. A bird of prey, blustered by the wind, soars above the valleys, its gaze focussed on finding movements in the grass. The scene stretches before us but we have to keep our eyes firmly fixed on the precipitous path which picks its way around the mountainside. It is probably a deer path, or one made by sheep; ice encrusted and covered in scree, it is not for the faint-hearted. Proceeding with caution and using sticks, we feel so small on this slope. The landscape seems to control us, its dark peaks towering above us, we are hostage to their height and vulnerable to steep descents. There is not a feeling of hostility, but one of indifference, as if the hard landscape didn't care. The fauna that feels at home here goes about its business without noticing us, the birds seem unbothered by the winter chill, although I am sure that finding food must be much harder in these cold conditions.

Fortunately nobody falls, and after the steep decline, a pub. The grey austerity of its outer walls and the dark tiles of its roof does it little justice, for it is welcoming within; a haven of hospitality with roaring fires, laughter and dogs. With whisky, we toast each other for completing our challenge. History seems to speak through the black beams and uneven plaster; stags' heads with monstrous antlers adorn every wall. Some tartan bagpipes hang on a hook as if awaiting a musician to conjure up a tune. One couldn't mistake this for being anywhere but Scotland.

A hearty and sustaining soup is welcoming. Through steamy window panes we watch the day close in with sullen petulance, mountain tops enveloped in pillows of grey. Here we will linger, in no hurry to leave. And when the whisky has worn off, we will find the car and drive alongside the loch a little, wondering what secrets it holds in its ink black depths. If the weather clears, the moon's face might stare into it, reflected in ripples as it did one winter some years before. And so with stomachs satisfied and feet and fingers warmed with a whisky glow, we will go to our beds to sleep away the winter night before another hiking day.

Sea myths

I am inspired by the sound of seals "singing", coming to the remote Scottish islands to breed in autumn and winter, their round blubbery bodies perfectly adapted to keep out the north-sea winter cold. Seemingly helpless on land, the pups shuffle pathetically about, looking up at everything and anything with limpid, trusting eyes which could melt the coldest heart.

The haunting songs of the seals are eerie, ethereal, bewitching. They presumably inspired the Scottish stories of selkies; seals which shed their skin to become human. Their beauty and form bewitched and beguiled humans, but it was often the human who would steal the skin of a female selkie and force her to marry him, even though she yearned for the sea. Attractive male selkies would be a wonderful distraction to lonely crofters, women who perhaps felt hopeless, helpless and a little empty as they watched over bleak and windswept winter landscapes and stormy seas, listening to the plaintive melodies of the seals coming in drifts from nearby beaches and wondering when and if their fisherman husbands would return home.

The ancient Greeks talked of sirens, similarly beautiful but dangerous, seductresses who sang with the sweetest sensual voices, causing enchanted sailors to shipwreck off rocky Grecian coasts. These birdlike women metamorphosed into the classic mermaid of medieval times, a woman with a fish tail. There is surely some similarity in these stories, stories coming across the centuries from different times and different parts of the world. It is of wonder that they might have been carried across the sea like messages in bottles. Perhaps these tales were carried by sailors themselves as they went from port to port.

In the small medieval church in the Cornish village of Zennor, the figure of a mermaid is carved into a pew. Slim-waisted and long-tailed, she holds a mirror in her hand. This is a standard image which I have also seen in medieval church wall paintings in another part of south-west England, but this particular mermaid is supposed to represent the beautiful Morveren. The legend states that the enigmatic Morveren would don a long dress to cover her tail and regularly visit the church for the Sunday service where she captivated church-goers with her ever-youthful beauty and her exquisite singing voice. The enigmatic young woman was not known in the village and vexed the villagers by her elusive presence for she never stopped to pass the time of day, but would slip away at the end of the service and vanish into the night. Either she was entranced by a young man called Mathew, who had the most rich and resonant male voice in the parish, or he was captivated by her charms, perhaps it was even a mutual attraction, a love at first sight. However the story is told, it is agreed that one evening he followed her out from the church, not only out of intrigue to see where she went, but out of desire. He never returned. It was said that he followed her to the sea, that their secret love was consummated and that many years later a sailor met a mermaid down at nearby Pendower cove, where he had moored his boat. She requested that he move his anchor as it was leaning against her front door. It was thereby deduced that this was indeed where Mathew now lived with Morveren and their children. The sailor, afraid of a mermaid's fickle nature that could turn like the sea and cause him to wreck his ship, obeyed her orders and left.

Although I can imagine Mathew's equally imaginary family, with their shipwrecked hearts, left standing on the cliff top looking down over the cove with its wild rocky outcrops onto which the winter sea slams, and wondering if their son still survived, it is more that this situation would have been a reality to the countless families of sailors lost at sea. Such austere rocks and petulant stormy seas in winter are the perfect places for causing ships and hearts to sink. It is no wonder that stories and legends abound.

The legend goes on to say that if one listens carefully on a winter's day, Mathew's voice will be heard singing in sonorous tones, warning sailors to stay snug at home and not attempt to go out into the wilds of a winter sea. I wonder if people had once heard the seals singing so long ago, for there are indeed grey seals in Cornwall no doubt inspiring stories. Legends they might be, but they contain some truth for surely they perhaps act as a warning against the dangerous and potentially destructive consequences of human nature; a nature that is impulsive, tempted towards beauty and mystery, with an even stronger inclination to follow the heart.

Sheep farm

One winter weekend we stayed on a sheep farm. The large rambling Georgian farmhouse, deep in Cotswold country offered comfortable beds, big breakfasts, and a guest living room with crackling fire and coffee table piled with books and board games to while away the winter hours.

We arrived at 4 o'clock, dusk drawing in. From outside, the farmhouse windows glowed. I could see the surrounding fields were full of sheep, their woolly forms fading into the backdrop of evening. We were welcomed with a pot of tea and homemade cake, chatting to the hostess who informed us that the sheep farm was a thriving business, lamb exported mainly to France. They feared Brexit.

After a few board games in the guest lounge, we set off for a country pub-warming winter food and a glass or two. The laughter of locals rang around the walls as they poured more pints. Last orders then back to bed, to a sleep which was the deepest and most dreamless that I have ever had while away, for normally I do not sleep well in strange places.

The morning arose cold and clear; after a big breakfast we went to see the sheep who stopped and stared, disconcerted; bulging eyes set in speckled faces. Some of them stamped their stick-like legs, an action which was comical. There is nothing scary about a sheep. Eventually they got used to us and resumed their grazing, picking through the snow-speckled grass. The wind was bitter but the golden morning light seemed to scintillate their fleece; thick fleece which would protect them through the cruellest cold. I hoped that after shearing, their wool would be collected and cleaned, dyed and spun as it was done in countless cottage industries up and down the country in the past. In present times there has been a resurgence for cottage crafts; an outlet for colourful creativity. The tide is turning and people prefer homemade, handmade, natural, organic and original. Machine made is out and hopefully with it acrylic; sticky, stifling acrylic which clings in overheated rooms and leaves so many microfibres in our washing water. I snuggle in my merino jumper; soft, warm and durable. I wouldn't want anything else!

In a country where artists and artisans are beginning to receive the recognition they deserve, along with farmers, I feel the tide is turning back in the right direction. In addition, diverse displays of items which have been carefully and lovingly prepared, are aesthetic and good for the senses. At a Farmer's market later, amongst the arrays of beautiful vegetables, homemade jams stood beside chutneys, crafted cheese and cider, there were cuts of meat, even hand-made goat's milk soap. The only plastic I encountered claimed to be made out of recycled bottles. People are turning to recycled, upcycled, reclaimed, vintage and antique. They take their own bags.

So back to the sheep; such is the simplicity of their lives that they do not have to worry about any of this. Their worries are only of strangers coming close to them, or of who will feed them. One of them bleated, breath curling in the cold, another answered, their calls carrying on the clear air until the whole flock were bleating. Then I saw the farmer, stomping across the field from one of the barns, carrying food. The animals instantly turned and moved towards him, as if in unison. Scampering, bundling and bumping, a big woolly flock, each wanting to be first to the food. They were pregnant and needed extra sustenance on such cold days, their unborn lambs no doubt made them hungry. And so they bundled and bumped and bleated some more and we watched them go, away through the sun-streaked morning as a papery moon faded into a clear blue sky.

Abroad

Istanbul looked serene that winter; a watercolour wash of empty streets subtly smudged with streetlight and shadows. As night drew in, the muted monochromes of a winter's afternoon underwent chameleon transformations; colours collided on wet pavements as lingering lights formed reflections which trailed with the blaze of comets. Men selling roasted chestnuts shouted on street corners, their produce exuding deeply rich aromas, coffee strong. We hovered around patisseries (pastanes), the allure of their windows golden and glowing, displays of baklava and other sweet and syrupy bakes stacked like pyramids too tempting to resist. The boza man cried in the empty streets, selling his ancient drink of fermented grains, considered a winter warmer. Yet most people preferred to huddle inside, crowding the cafes of the empty tea gardens. Shrouded in smoke from cigarettes and narghiles (waterpipes), they whiled away the hours while trams rumbled past outside, people pressed against steamy windows. Snow stung the sky in icy pellets falling between grey buildings and lethally icing the pavements where children slipped about and exchanged clandestine objects in dark alleyways and dejected dogs hung their heads in hope of bread.

Mornings were cold and grey, sitting beneath a sullen sky. Comfort came with a circle of sesame bread called simit, hot and fresh from the oven, sold on the street with a glass of tea. When not working, cold days were best spent ensconced in museums, fusing with time's tread, or else settling in a café with friends. The trees always looked on, their skeletal forms melding with the city mist. With them seemed to stir all the memories of a rich history, a legacy sleeping in the shadows while the city lay subdued in snow.

I left Istanbul to itself, a ghost city of empty streets, breathing its many memories while its citizens stayed inside overheated apartments. Deep in the Thracian country-side, wrapped in its blanket of snow, the silence echoed like light bouncing off brilliant white. And there we built a barbecue, my friends and I, cooking fresh fish and drinking raki which warmed first the throat, then the whole trachea, while the snow gleamed about us. It seemed slightly surreal to be having a barbecue in winter. And in the shadow of towering Thracian tumuli it felt historic somehow, as if ancient man were watching, remembering similar experiences from their shadowy tombs.

In Cappadocia it was as if snow had been sifted across the tufa from a giant sieve, the light dusting sugar-coating this dream world to make it magical. There is nowhere else on earth like it. Ancient monasteries cut into the rock speak silence, reassurance. They have been here for centuries, stilled by the breath of time. A rock dove cooed gently, its throaty warmth like honey, resonating in the stillness. Cave dwellings glowed everywhere, warm and welcoming. This is a place of stone, hard and yet forgiving, yielding to the desire for comfort from the cold. This is raw nature, an environment and landscape stripped to its bare bones, like the naked trees of winter. There are few trees here yet the rocks hold the same resilience, the same exposure to the elements, the overcoming of the harsh and cruel with a reassurance and comfort which makes all seem good.

In Greece, I also visited monasteries perched on the rocks of the Meteora. Living not far away, I would approach them from a village where wood smoke curled from chimneys and chickens strutted amongst skittering leaves. It was like a pilgrimage to the vast monasteries. Set upon their dark rocks, they seemed like distant glowing bastions on hostile crags. In winter the rocks seemed particularly foreboding; not only dark but snow-stippled and slippery.

Yet my friends and I would walk the two miles up the road from the village to the top, the breeze shuffling through leafless trees which had looked so beautiful in autumn, the air catching our breath in clouds. Sometimes we would be followed by a village dog, which barked and growled, making the refuge of the monasteries even more compelling. Himonas (χειμώνας) is the Greek word for winter, this onomatopoeia starts with a guttural Ch/h sound, stresses the second syllable and finally falls off the tongue. It is a word which I always find evocative of the season, making me feel deliciously uncomfortable and comfortable at the same time.

When cold and tired, we finally reached a monastery, we were always happy to be welcomed cordially by the monks as they ushered us into their glowing frankincense-spiced interiors which glittered with gold. Candle-light flickered across walls and fused with frescoed faces, faces appearing and receding in the guttering light. These were ancient frescoes, byzantine; the stylised faces of saints frozen in time as if they had been caught on camera all those centuries ago and still watched from the recesses of the great walls.

The monks live a simple life here, one

devoted to prayer and service to God. It is a life of self-sufficiency, not just through growing food, which must be particularly difficult in this rocky environment and especially in winter, but also by the fact that they have left their families and live an ordered and sacrificial life here as a community. Thus they require emotional resilience as well as physical stamina and I think of Cappadocia. But winter is all about resilience and stamina. It is a time of survival. It is a time when wildlife finds it particularly hard to find food, bracing against the cold, birds and animals go in search of what meagre morsels they can find. We so often associate winter as a time of feasting and merriment because it is our way of coping with the cold, of banishing the winter gloom from our lives, but the reality is frugality and scarcity. I imagine these monks live a frugal existence, one which they have chosen and which seems to make them happy. They have devoted their lives to the spiritual and this sustains them. Perhaps we all have too much, and material possessions and a fast life which leaves no room for reflection does not necessarily give us lasting joy.

New Year's Day

The coast road which dips and climbs through the West of Dorset is one of the most dramatic, boasting some of the most spectacular and panoramic views of many a road I have been on. In winter, however, it is prone to sea-mist and fog; heavy blankets of it rolling in like smoke. When travelling to Sidmouth to see friends one New Year's Day, the fog was so thick that it destroyed any visibility beyond a few metres. It felt as if we were entering an adventure, something unseen and unknown, which added to the suspense and the adrenaline of our journey. Our car was buffeted by constant cross-winds gusting in off the sea with considerable force. It was not really a day to drive any distance, but we were spurred on by the thought of arriving in time for tea and Christmas cake in a tiny, traditional fisherman's cottage, nestled in front of a roaring fire with our old friends and hearing the comforting echo of the waves crashing against the sea wall.

On that occasion, the waves were so high and spectacular, that we were compelled to leave the cosy fireside and brave the elements; walking along by the sea wall to get a better look and being blown so strongly by gusts of wind that we could hardly stand against it. This was a true display of winter wrath with its ship-wrecking storms. As we walked, we became more and more saturated by the slapping of sea water against concrete, riding up several metres in a torrent of spray which rained down upon us. It was dangerous and fun, but we still held a healthy respect for the sea that day, as it unleashed its power. Returning to the cottage at dusk, our tangled hair stiff with salt and our faces fresh and exhilarated, we were ready for a hot dinner eaten around a tiny table in the hall. A small, glowing Christmas tree winked warmly from where it stood on the foot thick window-sill which displayed the solidity of this old cottage. Its walls had withstood the centuries, witnessing many such storms, providing a welcome home and refuge to many a fisherman whose existence could be threatened by the fickle moods and the petulance of the sea. So this cottage exuded its timeless sense of safety, away from the wild echo of wind and wave, so that sitting comfortably around the table, which fitted snugly under the stairs, I had no wish to return home along the lonely, coast road, fog-muffled and buffeted by the storm.

MERLIN

A merlin suddenly swoops,
Entering our space
From a higher dimension,
Sharing a second with us
Before rising again.

It hovers
Endlessly,
A wizardry of precision
Holding us
Captivated,
Suspense savoured in the command of
concentration,
Each muscle motioned,
Positioned,
Poised above us.

And as it looks down,
Intently,
Suspended in silence,
Time seems to stand still.

Spellbound, we continue,
Wondering at its endurance,
Sharing its slow-motion suspense,
Not daring to move a muscle while it waits,
Hovering,
Holding a hypnotic gaze.

DAYS AND DREAMS

Dreams

I want to walk in the deep arctic tundra in mid-winter, savouring the sound of silence; that muffled stillness which breathes unabated across a white wilderness. This must truly be a wonderland; trees bearded with lichen and weighed down with a frost so thick that twigs and branches have become intricately iced like festive filigree decorations. This is the land where animals move secretly and noiselessly, the shadow of a lynx behind a blizzard, a wolf skulking away between the trees; only their paw prints giving away any clue to their presence. Despite the wild animals, in this dream I would build a fire and hunker down within the snowy landscape, watching the embers glowing in the deepening dusk.

The white unblemished purity of soft snow stretching forever, unmarred by man is surely something worth seeing. I have never seen snow so deep that it can be cut into blocks, like a knife through butter, dazzling in the sunlight of a shimmering day, white against blue like sugar-cube houses in the Mediterranean but with a brilliance which swallows shadows. An ice hotel would also be the place to stay; everything constructed from ice; imagination merging with creativity and taken to a new level, a level of complete amazement, a place where I imagine one is totally lost in wonder as one wanders around, gazing at glittering ice chandeliers, walking through ice arches into glowing ice rooms furnished with ice tables and chairs, decorated with ice statues....

And finally, as I stand in my dream world, the sky spreading above, the shifting shapes and patterns of the aurora borealis will move silently in mesmorizing formations above the frozen earth, ethereal and unearthly. Such natural beauty and wonder, such immensity of mystery and awe. I want to experience the stars out in that vast expanse, the Milky Way stretching its icy arm endlessly into infinity. And away from everybody on earth, I will look to the heavens and thank God.

Illusions

Winter now in Southern England is more often warm and wet; I crave the chill of childhood. However, hearing the patter of rain on the path outside the window is comforting, compelling. I have to go out. Walking in the wet woodlands is therapeutic. Raindrops patter into the last of the leaves which coat the forest floor; shiny wet the muted tones of brown, amber and orange have come to life in the glowering light. The day is drab, yet there are still signs of life, of texture and colour. A squirrel scampers up a tree and shrieks a rusty squeak, tail erect and quivering, wet light lingers on the tree trunks, and puddles on the pathway reflect the upside down umbrella forms of naked trees before a leaden sky.

A trail of painted pebbles follow the woodland path. I think of Hansel and Gretel. Children have certainly painted these pebbles; bright with rainbows and colourful, creative patterns. Their purpose is perplexing; something distinctly manmade in a wet winter wilderness, something artificially bright, bringing joy to a drab day. The stones peter out but the walk continues, rain ricocheting through bare branches, yet robins still sing, the brilliance of their song like polished copper ringing through the rain. Starlings join them with clicks and whistles, lifting the day to a new dimension.

Suddenly some toadstools, big, bright and perfectly domed. They look too good to be true, plastic in their perfection. The white spots are regularly spaced across a red background, shiny in the rain, they have not been bitten by anything but stand pristine, larger than life. This is a fairy tale forest of illusions, where mushrooms, perhaps "magic", appear larger than life and children's footsteps linger in a legacy of painted pebbles. Such colour and perfection on a dull day is unexpected. The toadstools, beguiling in their beauty, compelling in their perfection, tempt me to test them. Looking so real there is something strange about them, and although fungi are like alien beings, these are certainly not real. When I tap the top, my finger fails to yield to something soft, but hits a hard surface; plastic. Two small markers beside the toadstools suggest a miniature burial, perhaps a pet, deep in the forest. Like the pebbles, their story and their existence remains a mystery.

But winter is full of stories, told around a fireside on cold winter's nights, as we watch faces morph through flickering flames. Even though it is warm and wet, the comfort of storytelling still remains, and imagination runs wild with the inspiration which it chases between the trees.

Lewesdon

A day of deep sunshine; the sort that moulds itself into the earth with all its soft undulating contours and seeks to seep into every furrow of every ancient tree yet does not warm. Beech trees stand like soldiers along a medieval wood bank, the permanence of their presence juxtaposing the passing of lives through the centuries, people who once walked this same spot. Perhaps the trees remember, for they seem to breathe memories into the ancient landscape. There is an insane stillness in the sunshine while boot-wrenching, beech-masted mud sucks at our steps with a relishing slurp. We snatch them back, sinking and slipping, kicking up mounds of dry leaves. This is children's fun and I feel a generation younger, warm and energy-glowing despite the wind's cruel chill chastising knuckles and putting hands into pockets. Down in the valley, sheltered from the roar of the wind which rips through trees on the hilltop, the air hangs disjointed with fragments of bird-song. Sweet and sharp- their shafts of sound stab like the cold, yet reassure as life continues in this peaceful permanence and the trees look on, seemingly indifferent, having withstood centuries of seasons before.

Birdsong

The air is elastic as if stretched by the continuous clicking and chattering congregation of starlings which fidget in naked tree tops, the weather mild, even daffodils flower, trumpets opened in full force. On the grass verge a couple of herring gulls paddle their feet as if doing a tap dance. They are charming worms which during this dry spell have no doubt retreated to the depths of the earth. I am walking back from the corner shop on this warm early December day of wan sunshine, catching this few minutes of the natural world before I spend the afternoon inside caring for a convalescent. And suddenly I see my environment as through the bright eyes of a child, noticing the nature on our very doorstep, the warm comfort of being within the sphere of home. I stand in the garden listening. The chatter of starlings continues, the warm drift of a woodpigeon seeps through the stillness against the faint backdrop of people living their lives; a door banging, somebody laughing. More birdsong blends into the medley. I cannot identify each individual song but I know that the house sparrows were back this morning, winging through the garden with a thumbing-through-yellow pages flick. Suddenly the sun subsides and it begins to rain; a fine drift of mizzle and the birds are silenced. Now I hear the light, almost indistinct patter like a flutter of butterfly wings on the pile of dry oak leaves which litters the lawn. When the sun returns, so do the birds and the bright sphere streaks the sky with its setting hue so that the trees become silhouettes in the stillness and the day is done once more.

Under the sky

A day pregnant with clouds; swollen skies hanging heavily as if about to give birth to rain. A day non-descript, a lifeless landscape which seems ancient yet timeless. Today it feels ancient in an aged sense as if it were stuck in a state of lethargy, weighed down with the problems of the past. Grey and understated, bored of its many memories, it seems sunk in silence, depressed under heavy cloud and a gloom that fails to lift. None of this influences my mood, for wildlife provides constantly changing and unpredictable encounters, always lifting the day to a new dimension, and although I have walked here many times before, I am completely contented to experience the melancholy mood of this winter landscape and see something exciting within it.

Above the silhouettes of ash, whose leaves have long gone, leaving only bunches of keys, ash keys, to unlock a new life, a convoy of birds move in unison above the ancient forests and fields. One group meets another and they converge, combining in the air and moving on together. Snatches of their sound, wild and haunting, stretch across the open spaces of the sky. They rise and fall, moving in a unified, fluid formation for several minutes, disappearing and then reappearing until eventually they fade away.

Down a deep drove where midges meander aimlessly about our faces, gold-finch gather in winter trees, their bright feathers streaking against the sky as they take off and land. Sociably they converse, congregating in bushes and trees to feed before flying away in a flurry of gregarious chatter with a whisk of wing. They are not the same species as the birds which circled the sky earlier, neither were they starlings which congregate in the treetops, whistling and clicking.

Despite the fact that the countryside appears drab and desolate, many birds choose to overwinter here. The distinctive clacking of a male stonechat from the top of a bush reminds us that these small birds will brave the cold and continue to assert their territory with their flint rubbing rasp. Other birds from colder northern climes choose to overwinter in England. Redwings are one such bird that does just this and we spot a large group of these gregarious thrushes hopping through a field together, presumably feeding on the insects which they find. Their red underwings certainly give away their identity and provide brushstrokes of colour against the subdued wintry backdrop of chalky marls and muted browns. Fieldfares are another, larger winter migrant of the thrush family. Unless they were the birds which were flying together in the sky above, I have not seen any today.

As the various groups of birds cavort like children, the landscape remains unimpressed, locked into its lethargy, staying at a pace slower than the life which hurries about above and within it. We are merely walkers passing through, helpless to save the tired old year as it staggers to a close and ready to welcome the new rejuvenated one which will soon begin.

White doe

The enigmatic form of a white doe flicks between the trees; an elusive phantom presence passing before our eyes for a second before disappearing. Although a deer, she is no reindeer; and no animal such as her was present at the manger that precious night. Up here is blast bitten, the wind gnawing at fingers and faces, a frost carpeting the flat ground. Holly berries blaze in bushes and puffed up robins flit about, landing on any available perch to stop and stare with cocked-head beady eyes. There is little heat in the golden glissando of sunlight which runs unbroken across the treetops and over the sweeping stretch of heathland where the doe now grazes peacefully, timidly. She has every right to be timid for she is as bright as snow, no camouflage contains her. And while the wild backdrop echoes with the ethereal cries of wading birds wintering in the salt flats, she continues undisturbed. Then something startles her and in as brief an instant as a fallen snowflake, she has melted away.

Country walk

I step through frost-filled gullies where sunlight sparkles and where every dead leaf is given new life, each adorned with a glittering crystal coat which enhances its beauty and being. The forest is silent, slowly thawing as tongues of sunlight stretch between the silver wands of coppiced trees. It is waking from the wonder of a dream, the remnants of that wonder still all apparent in the glitter and glimmer of frost, the forms of leaves - each etched in ice, intricate, ornate in design.

A wren flicks through bushes, busy, irritable. A woodpigeon casts its creamy croon; its calm, melted-butter warmth lingering like the sunlight on tree trunks. The forest continues stirring from its slumber within the shadows of the dream world; a winter night when frost encased the earth with its shining armour making muddy paths strong, unyielding. Yet where the sun's melting breath has touched, these paths have awoken to become the reality of a clay quagmire through which wellies slurp and suck. And where the leaves have lost their silver coats, they become drab, lifeless, trampled down, defeated, only to be reclaimed as part of the earth.

After a country walk, coming back cold, wet or muddy, there is nothing better than a bath and baking. Before the walk, I concocted an apple cake, savouring the sweet butter and cinnamon aromas. It will now be delicious served with a cup of tea and a dollop of clotted cream.

By the sea

Down by the jetty a scurrilous wind whips walls and empty hulls with stinging projectiles of sand and spray. Waves spit their slander at the shore and hiss contempt at a wind-scurried seagull which cowers, buffeted by the blast, feathers flurried as it stands stoically looking out to sea. It wobbles with each gust, trying to balance on spindly legs.

Scouring winds skid across the surface of the sand, blasting puddles; their surfaces shrinking, shuddering. We wince at the punishment of the elements, for the wind is raw and merciless, the sea showing its strength as it flexes its muscles to strike ships. Many became wrecks in the past, plundered then swallowed up; their legacies left lost beneath the gut-wrenching swell.

The haunting cadence of the wind blows ghostly melodies through rigging, unleashing a vagrant melancholy, strange and whimsical in its otherworldliness. Brought back to earth by the continuous chink of masts, the thrump of flags being blown about, by the wild, mournful, wind-drowned calls of oystercatchers, I find something exhilarating in this atmosphere of juxtaposition. This is a place where inanimate becomes animated and the animated persevere stoically, intent on not being overwhelmed by the elements and the bitter blast of winter by the sea.

Wistman's wood

Fog hangs like lichen in Wistman's wood, shrouding troll-like trees in layers of mystery and antiquity. Hidden in the heart of Dartmoor, this place is eerily ancient, eerie in the sense that it is shrouded in silence. It has always been here, contained within itself for centuries, and is thought to be one of the most ancient fragments of native forest left in the UK.

We tread carefully across big boulders

of granite, called clatter, chaotic, cloaked in green and glaring in the lugubrious light. Silhouetted shapes of trees seem to feel their way through the fog towards us, like living beings with blindly groping limbs which reach out in crooked contortions, fingering the clatter. Moss, lichen and epiphytic ferns festoon these bare branches. Despite no leaves, all is green, dank and damp. Damp rises in the nostrils, the savour of mulched leaves lingers on the air.

Through the silence the occasional crack of a twig being snapped, the patter of a drop makes us jump. And then a blackbird breaks the silence with its clipping alarm call and then another, their sounds stabbing the stillness with echoes that seemingly dissolve into mist and time.

Time feels trapped here. As if it had stood still for centuries, fusing the present with ancient past. The oak tree's naked limbs reveal stunted features; twisted, grotesque yet strangely beautiful. Each is an individual, yet thriving as one entity in a rare and fragile ecosystem. These trees are, however, taller than they were some centuries before. Climate change; the world is now warmer.

I wonder at the age of some of the trees,

for which I hold deep respect. I find fascination in an organism which is still alive, having started as a sapling some 400 years ago, sprouted from the acorn of an ancestor which might have begun growing several centuries before that. So the trees of the past have left their legacies in the trees of today, which are still considered ancient. I cannot imagine what they have witnessed as times have changed, and yet in this woodland, the same scene has probably remained throughout the centuries with little change to note from day to day. Only the seasons marking time. Some of these trees have witnessed and withstood at least 400 winters. Their high altitude could make them vulnerable to storms but their low-lying squatting stature and their creeping limbs, which cling together in a confusion amongst the clatter, perhaps protect them.

Awe is not the word, and nor is wonder. I find these ancient places too big for me, too deep to suitably express. The connection with times past inaudibly rings around the forest, hanging as heavily as fog and the lichen bearding the branches of old oaks. Dartmoor is full of prehistory. Tumuli stud the landscape and ancient trackways trace the footfalls of prehistoric people. No doubt they were once in this very forest, those people, staring into its ancient heart as we do today. Did they stare with the same respect? For as some people still are, they were keen on deforestation. The moor was once wooded, completely cloaked in trees, or so I am told. Why this fragment was left untouched through time remains a mystery. Today it is significant for its age and uniqueness. Yet its preservation makes it seem as if it has always held something special, a significance which has changed through time and will probably never be known.

Beaver family

Beavers live in the same county as Wistman's wood. They were not reintroduced after an absence of 400 years, but found their own way here. In countries like Canada they are well adapted to winter conditions and prepare for them throughout the year. Creating cosy dams where they give birth to their young, it is wonderful to see a beaver family on a cold winter's day, huddled together deep beneath the branches which they have piled together. This has been shown on cameras which look into their private lives. Beavers also break off the branches of surrounding trees, dragging them to the dam entrance and burying them into the river bed as a winter food store to ensure survival.

Storm

The wind sends squalls, slaying the skies in driving, horizontal bands. Wind whipped trees writhe with its lashing force. Out in the fields where wind tousled tumuli rise, their round humps resisting the storm as they have done so many times through the centuries, all is bleak, the atmosphere ancient, strong in its survival against the elements. I walk near wind scoured puddles, their surfaces skinned by a flaying wind which sends shuddering sheets of water to skim the surface in a myriad minute wrinkles and ripples. All around me energy and exuberance of the storm, a wild power unleashed, a completely contrasting exuberance to when the blackbirds burbled their first notes two days ago, awakening the promise of spring. Now their melodies are silenced, yet excitement is not subdued but sustained in the energy of the moment, the comfort of being cosy in a padded anorak while the wind whips around. Spring will surely come eventually but this is the now to be experienced, to be savoured, a new invigorating experience which stirs the senses and allows us to partake more readily in the natural world to which we belong.

Penny whistle

Rain ricochets in empty streets, wan light plays in puddles as shadows pass. Water pours in pattering streams off gutters and awnings; soaking pavement and path.

Men in smart suits make a dash for it, some under umbrellas, others holding files, laptop covers, whatever they have, over their heads. Women accompany them in high-heels, not dressed for this weather. They are office workers rushing to buy lunch somewhere. In the square the taken-down Christmas tree stands forlorn, denuded and stripped of decorations. A few frail wisps of wind-torn tinsel linger, the last strings of extinguished lights flap frantically.

Through the patter, and high-heeled clicks, the drawl of buses and whip of the wind, come the shrill, bright notes of a penny whistle; the player, an elderly tramp, bundled in layers in a shop doorway. Protected from the rain, he plays his whimsical tunes, which trip and flow like clear streams despite themselves. Laughing eyes and lively fingers, there is also life in his lips as he plays, giving his whole heart and soul; music means everything to him at that moment, bringing joy to others. These are folk songs from the past; simple, joyful, sung by those who laboured the land, helping them to get through.

People walk past, preoccupied with what they will have for lunch. In their business attire, they anxiously rush for the pub. No one notices; nor cares. Their only objective comfort; to be out of the freezing rain. Yet despite the cold, this man's fingers move, dancing with dexterity. He tongues out his tune, eyes smiling, crinkling at the corners. I give him some bright pennies, a pound or two for his trouble and perhaps for his lunch, some pennies for his penny whistle. He nods yet hardly notices; so engrossed in his world of jubilant melody, brightening a dreary day. It is perhaps not the money he wants after all. As I walk on, his notes ring as earworms, infectious in their enthusiasm; skipping and tripping despite the rain.

Looking into ice

The rain froze one night, spitting against the window panes with a callous, chaotic patter while the wind roared. Cradling cosy cups of cocoa, we warmed ourselves by winking firelight. It was the next morning that I was greeted by the glare of unmanufactured frosted glass as I crept into the pensive grey glow of a dawn-lit kitchen to boil a kettle and prepare porridge. The world was muted, still, locked outside so that I could only perceive it through its glint and glare. Steely, slumbering white whispers; I couldn't see the snow but envisaged the Arctic as I snuggled deliciously deeper into my dressing gown. The ice made modern art that morning; bas-reliefs etched with wandering lines and spiked with crystals, shadows sculpted in the flowing, frozen contours. It became a new part of my photographic portfolio as I delved deeper into the mundane, the seemingly obvious, to reveal ever more.

Across the fields

I hang back, while the others walk ahead, and savour the silence. In the stillness of this valley, soaked in winter sun, all is completely calm. Sheep graze with early lambs, the occasional bleat echoing across the valley. A clamour of corvids, jackdaws I think, stab at the silence as they jostle in a nearby copse and the sun sinks down, casting its golden glow across grass and treetop. Looking back at the horizon, I watch white horses riding on the distant blue spill of sea, cavorting with a callously cold wind which stirs its surface and causes the "horses" to toss their manes in streaks of spindrift. Another winter day winding down, yet each becoming longer so that soon we will see the days drawing out and lingering in the light of evening.

Landscape

Snow-stippled fields form the backdrop to a white-washed landscape. The transformation of the fields and everything round about is fresh, surprising so that we do a double take, marvelling at its new found beauty as we might when a girl grows up and one day appears all made-up and radiantly glowing. So it is with sunshine on snow. Fields shimmer in the golden light; boundaries and contours defined by the dark lines of hedgerows, the clumps of trees as if pencilled in. A flock of sheep, fleece blushing in the sunlight, stand softly against the snow, trying to forage frozen grass blades from the icy earth.

As the sun climbs above the snow-covered ridge, shadows seem to fall, tumbling down its ski-slope sides; the lengthened lashes of coppice clumps sweeping the slopes like brushstrokes, the long fingers of individual trees pointing into the shadowy valley where more snow has settled.

The wind is chill and biting, yet the sky holds a cloudless brilliance, a luminescence which expands into its ever upward sphere. Birds of prey glide the thermals, their victims surely more visible on the snowy backdrop. From the top of the ridge, where the icy wind blows so that our faces freeze with an after-dentist numbness, the views across the lowland heath draw our eyes upwards to horizon's higher levels where it wears white caps.

This is the view from Ballard Down looking over and across Studland, the blue of the bay curved and constant, the purple, brown and golden spread of heathland as the eye draws into Dorset and the legacy that the snow has left.

Coming out of the cold

The sun sculpts a new landscape during the golden hour. The heathland; uniformly brown at this time of year, blushes bronze, the white gold of silver birch trunks standing out slim and sleek in the mellowing light. The evening cuts a clarity as bright as the birdsong, speaking out against the wintery cold which seeks to spite us with its sharp breath this weekend. It is radiant now; a buoyant brilliance full of hope and joy and although still slightly cold, it is as if winter has turned the corner into spring. I worry for these birds who, beguiled by the brilliance of the evening and the warmer temperatures of the past weeks, could suffer if snow comes as promised. It is almost as if nature is playing games, a seductress who tempts then turns.

Winter

Harsh haw frosts
Cause cattle's curling breath
To trail on frozen foggy mornings.

A silver beaded spider's web
Caught by cutting breeze
Trembles.

Frail fields
Blanched in strained sunlight,
Speckled with sheep.

Nights draw in early,
Goose wings beat
Before a draining sky.

Candlelight dances in dusk-drawn ancient
churches,
Causing cold stone
To seep security.

Expectant childish faces
Steam windows
As they wait long hours

Lovers linger
Beneath berries
Of mistletoe
A pearly shell
Sighs
With secrets of the sea

And when the snow falls finally,
White upon white,
Silence echoing silence
Excitement can no longer be contained.

THOUGHTS AND REFLECTIONS

Streams of consciousness

I love my local beach in winter; drawn to its muted palette and its many moods; for even when the sun shines, the lower light gives less intensity, drawing longer shadows in the sand, leaving deep dimples and ripples around the dunes where the shadows swim in a golden lagoon of light.

On bright, fresh mornings such as these, the day can delude us; the dancing sunlight on the sea, the scintillated spume which washes in and in, skittering across the sand, chasing unsuspecting seagulls as the wind blows its elastic froth; all seems so inviting. And yet, that resonant blue water holds a chill which only those with wetsuits might dare to challenge, and the wind bears a bite which gnaws at hands and feet, leaving them throbbing.

On other days, blasted by the chill, a surly sea, tossed about by the wind, thunders onto the shore. It is the deep intensity of its roar, its cavernous rumble which enlivens even the dullest of days. With power unleashed, it states its presence on vacuous, non-descript winter days. The sand lies littered with shells, debris, and detritus from the sea. Tangles of bladder-wrack form a line where the tide turned. For a beachcomber or an artist, this holds hours of intrigue and curiosity; textures and patterns, the ever-varying shades of grey. This is a grey which is alive and thriving in its shifting state, not drab and vacant.

It is best to embrace days like these, to experience them. When shut inside, as we so often are, we incline to apathy and going out becomes an inconvenience. But once we greet the cold and start to look into the day and all that it holds in the natural, a whole spectrum of possibilities opens up, a plethora of experiences and distractions.

Running along the empty shoreline, that

vast space spreading like a blank canvas before and beyond, I wonder what the year ahead will have in store. As I hear the reassuring resonance of the sea spilling its secrets, I hope that the good things will not change. And as gulls pick at the treasures which the waves have left on the sand - gifts from the sea - I know we need not worry; everything can be provided. Days like this are free. Snug inside myself as the heat generated by running kills the cold, and the warmth of lovely thoughts seeps into the soul, I am alone with the sea's soliloquy and the joy of its sound, the feeling of freedom in a winter wilderness, left to my own thoughts. I run alone, but even if running with another, we do not talk much on days like this, but remain caught in contemplation, for the atmosphere is too vast, the day too deep. Only a handful of dog walkers share the shore this morning; they mind their own business, each lost in their own reverie. Winter makes one pensive, but not introspective.

Footprints in fresh sand show that others have been here before. A scatter of paw prints and the skittering marks made by birds. There are no bare human footprints on the beach today, but only boots with treads, deep treads which displace wedges of wet sand where someone has drawn patterns, perhaps to mark the winter dawn.

There are naked footprints on the beach far away at Formby; prehistoric prints of man, woman, child, walking there all those centuries ago, making their mark. Soon the prints will be washed away, their legacy left only to memory and imagination. Another set of family footprints were found on the Norfolk coast; apparently the oldest outside Africa. This ancient and long-forgotten family were perhaps foraging, like the gulls. Despite the millennia, their footprints provide something tangible, an ancestral connection through time. They experienced the same sea and seasons, the same hunger and cold, which they had to endure. We often think of those distant, intangible times as hard, grey, stoic like stone. We tend to think of them closer to the ice age, especially when we find remains such as those of the prehistoric hunter, frozen for five thousand years on an Italian mountain top until the ice eventually melted. There are dinosaur prints near the beach where I run on the Dorset coast; huge feet pressed into the stone, which must have been mud during those primeval days. I cannot imagine a world with those creatures, yet their presence is pervasive all along this Jurassic coast as the cliffs and rocks expose secrets, giving up the bones of buried dead. My mind is running races around and around, creating its own patterns, its own trains of thought. This is what winter does. It allows one to escape into streams of consciousness.

And so, my run complete, I head off the beach, skipping over the mini surfboards of cuttlefish carcasses which lie strewn and scattered everywhere, brilliant white. Razor clams are cast away beside them, the same shells which fascinated me on winter walks in childhood and which as an adult we hardly pay attention to. I am leaving the beach, drawn by the smell of wood smoke and baked bread; a beach café somewhere is setting up breakfast with all its comforting coffee aromas. If I were with my running partner, we would stop and grab a coffee now. Instead I head home; one last look back. The beach remains empty, chill, cheerless grey and pallid, uninviting yet strangely attractive, for I have already embraced it. Warm and energised, prepared mentally and physically, I can take on this wintery weather and conquer the coming day.

Winter sensations

I think perhaps winter is the most sensual of seasons in that it draws us into itself, wrapping us in its warm blanket and captivating us like children. There is the delicious cosiness of coming in from the cold, the tingle of fingers as they "thaw" in artificial heat. Man has always made fire to keep himself warm; the soot in prehistoric caves giving testimony to the brilliance of the firelight with its warm winking gestures bringing comfort and joy. Stories were once told around such flickering firelight and experiences were shared, as they are today in cosy country pubs with open hearths.

Food plays another very important part of winter; food to warm and sustain us, food for joy and celebration. Mulled and spiced, infused with flavours and fragrances, it is that special feast which we might not indulge in at other times of the year. For this is a time for festive fun and dazzling parties, a time for love and laughter spent with loved ones and a time to share and give.

Outdoor Christmas markets create a cocktail of sounds and smells; street food aromas mingling with mulled wine, beer and twinkling lights. There is the bling and the glitter, the tacky tunes contrasting the voice of a melodic choir. The sound of merry making and laughter, of people having fun flows through the evening air. The atmosphere is electric, ecstatic.

Then there is the silence; the strongest sound of all. For in the silence we still ourselves. In the long dark nights, silence rebounds in the iridescence of the moon and the shifting shadows. It stands in ancient places, the vast and lonely countryside, black beneath the sky's stretched canvas. There is the silence of a winter beach which echoes only with the sigh of the sea and the waves' metronomic wash. Snow is silent as it falls, layer upon layer, muffling the air around it, drawing in the breath of anticipation, of waiting for another year, a new beginning...

Masquerade

Things are sometimes not as they seem in winter; as if they were almost endowed with an alchemy which makes them marvellous. These things are often considered unremarkable at other times, but to a child at Christmas, the simple always seems fantastic. While we feigned sleep, my brother, cousins and I, it was with a bittersweet mix of excitement and fear that we heard the crinkling and crunching at the end of our beds and dared not peep. Hearts pounding, hands clammy, cramped, with muscles tense, we dared not sleep, yet dared not stir. Overexcited, we wondered if we were actually dreaming, only to wake in the weak shadows of extreme tiredness to see the bulging shape of a stuffed stocking and become overwhelmed with wonder.

It is the same wonder and delight that peers into the kaleidoscope which was placed in that stocking of discovery. The infinite shifting shapes and colours coming together, colliding and moving away in an endless symmetry of fascinating optical illusions. It is the excitement of opening the Matryoshka, or Russian doll; exotic with her painted red attire, stylised, blushing face with jet black eyes, to discover another smaller and then another, as if unwrapping the layers of a never ending parcel and wondering what the next will reveal. Our minds might associate Russia with winter fairy tales. It is also a land of shimmering snow and sledges and reindeer herds, a tundra full of towering trees and the Nutcracker. As we crack nuts in a bowl by the fire, Russia remains a land far away, an intrigue outside the realms of personal experience.

The final winter wonder pulled from my stocking; a snowstorm in a glass bubble, into which I gazed endlessly, entering a microcosm of houses clustered together as if providing warmth from the chill. And I wondered what it would be like to live there in that tiny community, cosy and contained, ready to assist each other when the snow was shaken down. To my idealistic child's eye, sitting in the comfort of my sitting room with my family around me, communities were always like this and people always helped each other.

What a wonderful world winter can paint; a world of harmony and containment, when things fit together so perfectly in colour, shape and size. These worlds can be entered into and explored so that the imagination is held completely captive while outside in the real world, the cruel, harsh realities seemingly cease to exist.

Pantomime

The excitement of the stage is not only confined to childhood, and the pantomime surely appeals to all generations. But I think to a child, there is that extra element of excitement and suspense. As a young child, I found the pantomime a place of contrast and illusion, a place which I did not perhaps totally understand and so held a love hate relationship with it. I loved the larger than life characters, the bright and dazzling costumes, the false voices, the silly songs. I loved the fact that there was audience participation and that the whole theatre felt involved and united against the villain or the baddy of the show. But I didn't always understand the innuendos, the adults rocking with laughter at some satirical aside which went over my head. I didn't always understand why some of the actors were so much larger than life, wearing an excessive amount of makeup, masks and wigs so that they resembled the fictitious characters in fairy tales. I also found it strange that the traditional fairy stories that I knew and loved had been twisted, distorted, presented in a different way; there was always an element of surprise. Yet winter is all about wonder and surprise, things which are not as they seem. The grotesque side of pantomime is seen in winter trees by moonlight, when they take on gnarled and contorted faces. It is reflected in the faces of gargoyles picked out by floodlights on a cathedral in winter. The grotesque also appears in fire-light when elongated shadows distort the features of even the most beautiful faces;

eyes become cavernous hollows and noses large and intrusive. I wonder if winter was part of the inspiration behind fairy tales, because they are often set in winter forests and always contain elements of ugly versus beautiful, the fantastic and the unexpected such as the story of Red Riding Hood and the Wolf, Beauty and the Beast or the Frog Prince.

As adults, of course, we know that all this is comedy and illusion and do not take it seriously, but as a child I found the faces a little disturbing, a bit like Punch and Judy. Fairy stories instil stereotypes into our psychology which are only erased as one gets older. So as a child I laughed but did not quite trust or understand the figures on the stage, I only trusted them because the adults were having so much fun, fully content to spend a few hours at the theatre in order to escape the winter blues.

As well as being full of fantasy, shock and surprise, the simplicity of the panto-mime perhaps also appeals, for there is something so unsubtle. It is a place of impulse and improvisation where characters are exaggerated, characters who one either loves or hates. Accentuated expressions and emotions reflect the faces of the firelight; simple storylines and slapstick humour contrast subtle innuendo. There are the direct contrasts of good versus bad, love versus hate, yes versus no, and for a child, the feeling of warm comfort of being with your family contrasting the fear at a sudden shout from the stage. The contrasts go on, but all add to the sense of surprise and confusion, the sense that nothing seems to be what you would expect. With its colour, comedy, chaos and character, the pantomime is part of the brightening up of winter and we shout lustily, escaping into the realm of fantasy and fun, becoming part of the show. For winter is a show, a spectacle, a world of wonder, illusion and bright diversity for those who wish to stave off the melancholy of the dark and cold.

Charades

Miming, it would seem, has always been a part of winter. In previous centuries, mummers would roam from village to village, dressed as strange characters and performing a play in friends' houses. The people of the house had to guess the identities of the mummers beneath the costumes. Also often played during the 19th century and even today during the festive season, is the game of charades. Full of fun and laughter, it enables everybody to let go of inhibition with the people they trust, and to experience something of the real self. We mime a book or a film, step into a different role. Yet what is a charade really? A pretence, a pretending to be someone who we are not, acting in a way which is untrue to ourselves. We often see ourselves as we want the world to see us and yet by others we are perhaps seen in a completely different light. Even if we pretend, convincing ourselves that we are someone other than we are, those who we allow to be close know our true self and nothing can be hidden from them.

Windows and doors

I am drawn to the deep reflections and glittering lights of windows in winter. The window; an eye into the interior which fills us with intrigue as to what lies within. Glowing interiors with the warm wink of lights naturally attract us. Shops, pubs and tearooms have worked this to an art and on this twilit evening in a small touristic village, it is the shop windows that coax me with their warm welcome. I do not enter the shops themselves straight away; for as with a beautiful present, too lovely to unwrap and so intriguing that we want to wait awhile and guess the contents, I stand outside for a while, savouring the anticipation and wondering what might be within. Sometimes I even have to imagine what sort of shop it might be or to what type of people it might appeal. A shop window filled with the grotesque faces of Pelham's puppets alongside a Jack in the Box, stuffed soft toys, a rocking horse, a beautiful dolls' house with Christmas tree all lit up, and a traditional Father Christmas brings back to me a childhood Christmas. For a child this place is an emporium of wonder and delight. Yet for the child of a past generation it would perhaps have more appeal than for the child of today, for there are no electronics here or screens. These toys are traditional, made with dedication and high-quality craftsmanship. It is as if we were travelling back in time to when my parents were small.

Then there is the sweet shop; striped sugar candy and traditional jars; again as if we had time travelled and once again a delight for children. Gold glints in another window. Handmade jewellery, original in execution and design, individually crafted expressions of enduring love. I wonder who will buy them this Christmas. The final shop window is full of crafts; ceramics creatively displayed alongside strings of lights, the theme silvery and snowy, perhaps the ceramics were made especially for the winter season. Some of the bowls are filled with red berries and draped with gold and I am excited by the aesthetic and the individuality.

Pubs and cafes similarly excite with their glittering Christmas lights, a roaring fire, a Christmas tree all glimpsed through large bay windows. Stands of cakes adorned with holly-sprigs, arrangements in evergreen and berry placed along windowsills. This is surely a warm welcome after a long country walk in the winter wind and relative "cold". Passing cottages with glowing windows hung with glass baubles and snowflakes, or the tall bow windows of large Georgian houses elegantly swagged and with an equally elegant Christmas tree glittering in its recesses. It is the comfort the homeless and less privileged crave. It is the transferred comfort which even as I stand outside, seeps into my bones and makes me deliciously warm.

It is the Georgian houses which always appeal to me the most but especially at Christmas. There is a grace and symmetry about their design, a gentle reassurance, a homely benevolence that states that all is alright in the world, all is in order and at peace. Perhaps I am biased because my grandparents lived in such a house and once we had passed through the beautiful recessed door with its carved doorposts, pediment and fanlight, we entered a simple, peaceful haven of comfort and security; of warm fire and ticking clock, of cooking smells and hearty meals, of intriguing nights in bedrooms full of interesting books, sweet sleep in immaculate, fragrant beds and always the softly lingering fusion of beeswax, polish and pot-pourri.

The door is the portal to the heart. A place of welcome, inviting people to step over the threshold into your private world and allowing them to see and share something of your life. It is where you lay yourself open, make yourself almost vulnerable by showing your inner sanctuary and pouring out love and friendship in your service to another person in order to make them feel comfortable and secure. It invites joy on meeting and sadness at parting, for it is the place for both. One of my longest lasting memories is of my two dear grandparents standing at their Georgian front door and waving to us as we drove off after a weekend visit. My loving grandfather had such a kind face, always smiling despite being sad to see us go (he usually cried before we left). For us children, he always ensured that our fists were filled with sugared almonds to be consumed on the journey home.

At Christmas time, nothing excites me more than a grand Georgian door decorated with a Christmas wreath. It is, to my mind, the height of aesthetic and I marvel at the creativity and individuality in each design, set off so beautifully by the door frame and fanlight. This Christmas I have been indulging in the sheer pleasure of observing people's doorways (and especially the Georgian ones!)

Both windows and doors display an array of creativity which seems to come to light at Christmas more than at any other time of the year. It is almost an act of love; something made carefully by hand to bring joy to others, to welcome them on winter days. It is good, in these days of machine-made commercialism, to see people turning their hands to something so beautiful. Despite it perhaps being an act of love, part of the physical beauty might be that it will not last forever and with it is an ethereality which makes it more precious because we do not take it for granted. Yet the love will last and the warmth will linger in our memories long after the winter has passed.

Those shared experiences when we paused at the window and then stepped over the threshold, passing through the portal into people's lives or when they passed through our portals, will go on. The joy of giving and sharing, of serving and making people feel welcome, loved and accepted is surely a message of winter with its decorated doors and glowing windows and should be a message which lives in the hearts of people throughout the year. A love which lasts forever and which, like the Olympic torch, can be passed from heart to heart through its welcoming warmth, a firelight flame which will never grow cold or be extinguished.

Support structures

Recently I passed a field where empty seedheads stood against a sweep of sky. They are the spokes of inside-out umbrellas battered by storms; denuded features in a gestating landscape where shaken seeds have freely fallen and lie, cosseted by the earth. I love the stark exposure of winter, revealing structures which support eco-systems and hold lives together, for in summer, flowers provide the framework for pollination, frequented by butterflies and bees and the food chain continues.

Now they stand as stalks with a symmetry of structure which once helped to hold flower-flourished heads high.

Naked hedgerows, which bear blossom in spring and berries in autumn, barely provide winter pickings. Birds rustle in leaf litter beneath them, stirring sudden movements in the still, grey lethargy of the day. Winter is mild these days and non-descript. This hedgerow, although still sheltering life, reveals only bare bones like carrion picked clean, a skeleton of its former self awaiting rejuvenation and resurrection with the coming of spring.

As hedgerows and wild flowers are so vital for the natural world, so are trees. I prefer them in winter, for without their crowning canopies, they show something of themselves, with the bearing of their branches they display each imperfection and idiosyncrasy of form. They lift up their arms to heaven and the birds sing in their shelter. There is a joy even in winter, always hope. The vast tracery of branches above is but a mirror of what stretches deep down into the soil; wandering root structures which not only provide a support network of communication to surrounding trees but support, as foundations, the whole towering tree itself. The tree in turn, in the fabric of its form, supports so much life.

In dormancy, trees become better known somehow, showing the true structure of themselves. Likewise, through its sleeping vulnerability, the landscape draws an intimacy. This is also true of relationships. We tend to hide beneath leaves, using them as barriers, hiding our faults and insecurities, not allowing our true structures to be exposed. Yet perhaps only when we have deep roots and can happily share our vulnerabilities, can we then support others.

Exposed

When winter storms cause the cliffs to crumble and white horses to canter to the shore, it is the best time to find fossils. The cliffs along the Jurassic coast yield an endless supply; creatures which have lain undiscovered, encased in their stone tombs for millennia. And so after a storm the fossil hunters come, frantically sifting through sand and shingle, smashing open stones to steal their secrets. If these fossils are not found before the tide rides in, they will be lost beneath the waves, washed away forever with no hope of ever being known. The thought of anything ancient and certainly something significant being lost to sight or science is too terrible for me, for there might be something as yet undiscovered, another piece of the puzzle which scientists are piecing together. Although people have found rare dinosaur bones and fossilised insects here, I have unfortunately never found anything unusual. Yet the thrill of finding any fossil has always been one of the most exciting experiences; the fascination of finding something so old and perfectly preserved, holding it in my hand and thus drawing a physical connection with a time so seemingly intangible that I wonder what the world was like when it was alive, indeed when its species still existed.

The cliffs also yield a wealth of intrigue to archaeologists, even if the finds might be more sinister, for when winter storms are severe, so severe that they cause excessive erosion, the cliffs are inclined to share secrets of the human dead. In 2014, for example, bones, thought to have been the burials of shipwrecked sailors, were exposed in the cliffs in Cwm Nash in Wales. More bones found in a cliff at Burrow Island, Portsmouth are thought to have been those of prisoners of war buried in the late 18th or early 19th century. These rather grim finds nevertheless provide another piece of the puzzle of history, another piece which helps to complete a picture of the past. The winter, through stark exposure of the elements, once again exposes, sheds light on the shadows. This is a season so candid that it can be read like an open book.

Reflection

Winter: the world has wound down, landscapes laid bare and trees ticking over. Evenings are long and lazy curled up in front of fires, the impish forms and faces of long licking flames curling and climbing as if trying to break free from the confinement of the hearth. The Christmas break provides the chance for winter walks in a pensive patchwork-quilt landscape which lounges in its dreamy comfort like long lazy mornings. It is time to slow down, to reflect, to move on from the old and prepare for the new.

Another year and the landscape continues to travel through time, never looking back. To trees, our lives are as frenetic as insects buzzing about, never sitting still. They seem so short as the tree stands stoically through the centuries observing time passing, the comings and goings. There is no real time. All is relative, moreover perceived. For although there are always 24 hours in a day, winter with its longer nights seems slower, steadier. We can relish and appreciate this pace for there is always time to be busy and never enough to pause and wait.

Seeing snow

Sinking into snow, footsteps muffled in a compressed crunch which seems to draw me down deep into itself, into its world. And through my macro, a whole new hemisphere is opened up to me, new dimensions displayed in the intricate individuality and elaborate design of the flakes which fall. So caught up am I with their revelation that I fail to feel the cold which crafts them. Each is unique yet sharing a six-sided symmetry. It is the way in which water molecules unite when frozen, yet as they fall freely through the atmosphere, each is shaped, sculpted by its individual journey like life's lessons shaping us. And as I watch the filigree forms fade and melt away, I also see life's transience.

These are like gifts from God; heaven-sent manna drifting down, opening my eyes. In their perfection they seem to reflect a perfect place beyond, where transience becomes permanence and the small and fragile become strong and inde-structible, and where there is a Designer so creative and caring that even the tiny and inanimate, which I cannot truly appreciate without my macro, is considered impor-tant enough to form.

Snowdrops

Snowdrops; the harbingers of spring still set in winter, and on a crisp, shining afternoon we watch lines of light and shadow play across the drifts of white. Despite there only being snowdrops, not snow, there is a feeling of ice on the air, as if it could come. Yet the brilliance of blue in the clarity of sky and air, the golden winter sunlight, falling on the furrowed trunks of ancient trees, and great-tits and blue-tits singing in their branches brings a buoyancy, an exuberance, a false sense of security.

The shy demeanours of snowdrops, bowing bashfully beneath the trees, petals tightly closed to form pure drops, are like nuns in prayer. Yet when they open up, lifting their veils, like little ears, they seem to be more alert and quietly listening. They listen to the conversation of the stream; water ice-cold, clear and pure. They listen to the whispers of the wind drawn through the still skeletal trees, the clandestine creakings and groanings of bare branches as trees respond in echoes. They listen to the distant bleat of sheep guzzling greens in a field nearby and the cow whose fog-horn call rings out across the valley, and with their small green eyes, perhaps they even see us marvelling at their understated beauty.

Light

I want a bright funeral
Flooded by the Light
That penetrates the inner soul,
Purging the velvet gloom
As it entered the world
One Christmas.

When I entered the world
My canvas was blank,
A white wonderland waiting before me.
Shivering on the threshold of infancy,
I took tentative steps in the snow
And fell.

I tried to paint the perfect picture
But life isn't like that.
My canvas blotted and blotched,
Was marred by the tread
Of time.

Only the Light
Can erase these steps
And show me the path
Which I should take
So that the canvas cleansed,
On the threshold again,
I stand and see.

NIGHTS

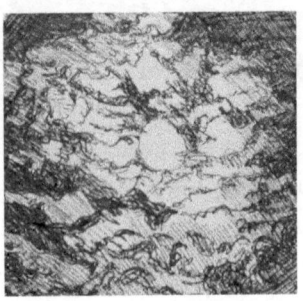

Homeward

The wind whipped through the trees last night, sending shadows to skitter and shift in pools of lamplight and whisking oak leaves into a delightful dance. They circled and twisted, caught in cold corridors of air, rising before they fell like raindrops, flicking my face with an expended energy, a candle burning out. Then with a slow sigh they finally sank to the soil to rest. In the morning, a filigree of frost picks out the curved lines and veins of these leaves which lie abandoned where the wind left them.

By the stream

The evening breath is cold and hard as it hangs in the evening. Skeletal trees are backed by a sinking sky of deepening dusk-grey and as day draws down to night it is chipped and chiselled with the blackbird's bedtime chide from somewhere within the dark lattice of interlocking branches. Rain patters in the soaked swathes of fallen leaves, the tributary roars; a full-blooded vein of water coursing and frothing and yet, on a gate post all is still and a female blackbird, fluffed up against the cold, sits looking out across the blank canvas of an open field, perhaps waiting for the sky to sink away into the depths of night.

Once home, we sit snug inside listening to rain ricocheting through trees, pattering on windowpanes. The night savours suspense in every drop, and in every silence when holding its breath before the wind is unleashed with a roar. Branches sigh in sympathy; a comfort to those creatures which use them as a refuge, sitting out the storm as best they can. The storm subsides eventually, lingering in the litter of leaves and in the leftovers of twigs and broken branches which are strewn haphazardly, saturated and forlorn, on pathways the morning after.

(Castleman Trailway, Dorset)

Dusk

We walk in the fading light. A fraying pink ribbon is all that is left as the sun stains the sky behind silhouetted trees and gives way to a refracted moon; a smudge in the evening sky. Light cloud is languid like the evening yet a pheasant runs in a demented fashion across a stubble field and a pigeon wings into the air with whistling flap. It is as if both birds are hurrying homeward. Chill air faintly billows the breath of cows which stand stoically, grazing in the half-light, their large black bodies pressed into the growing gloom. Sound sifts gently through the evening, a breeze breath through branches, so that a waiting stillness hangs over the countryside like a large yawn inviting all to hunker down as day drifts into night and daylight creatures yield to the darkness, snuggling beneath bushes or even in the earth. Starlings chatter in treetops, savouring the last light, like those taking last orders at the pub or ready-for-bed children in front of a screen which is about to be switched off.

Past the farm, where warming trails of sweet meadow hay and spiced wood smoke waft cosy comfort into the grey gloom. The hay holds in its every bale, the energy of sunlight and summer, a golden legacy stacked as food for overwintering livestock who cannot gain the nutrients they need from grass at this time of year. From the farmyard comes the evening call of a cockerel. It carries on the air, following us for some time, and blending with the deep-drawn hush of evening. Earlier the repeated ring of shot had echoed through the stillness, a parade of cars parked by the woods suggesting a hunt. Perhaps that was why both the pigeon and the pheasant seemed so edgy earlier.

Once the sky is sufficiently dark, the birds roosting and the cows slumbering in their shed, the stage will be set for a new round of nocturnal players; badgers snuffling about the abandoned copses, foxes furtively hunting. Yet even before they are about, there is the life which continues regardless of day or night. Strange fungi rise like fairy castles clinging to contorted tree trunks. They live out their strange and secretive existence, mysteriously and magically compelling, for one day they are here and another they are gone. It is said that some species even glow in the dark. These fruiting bodies are the part of the organism which is shown to the world. Under the ground they spread networks of hyphae which interact, helping to create, in most cases, a flourishing eco-system in the world above the soil.

We walk to an ancient hillfort where a wraith of mist rises, enigmatic and ethereal, hovering above the ramparts, tumuli and the landscape beyond; silhouetted trees become enfolded by the lowering light, a glimmer of the misty moon flicking through their bare branches. A feeling of powerful permanence pervades the stillness, the atmosphere strangely exciting. I imagine the ancients here sitting beside flickering firelight, perhaps telling stories inspired by their surroundings, and watching the flames casting shadows deep into the night. *(Dorset)*

Outside

I am caught in a web of fairy lights, of coffee-close bars and the tangled threads of conversations. Somehow I've been attracted to their sweetness, their stickiness like a fly to a fruit. It is cosy, chocolate-contented, yet I want to break free from its stifling clamour. Wrapped in endless empty conversations, we talk about everything and nothing. It is the same that goes around and comes around. Gossip draws me in with its sticky, deadly threads, tying me until I have to break free and go outside.

Out into the stark reality of night. The cold catches my breath. Beneath the quiet and shimmering expanse of stars, the full face of the moon as bright and crisp as the cold liberates me. An owl calls out of nowhere, perhaps hiding in a tangle of thicket. I listen to the hushed silence of the night, leaves falling like whispered words dropped casually from conversation. An almost imperceptible rustle in the undergrowth and the starry expanse stretching on and on to the deep unknown. All holds a breath-taking mystery.

This puts all into perspective. The burr of conversations coming from the pub fade into insignificance and I am alone with the night. The chatter of a stream somewhere deep in the darkness holds more meaning, the gentle gleaming eyes of a pony; its shape, dark in the shadows. Above, the stars spear the sky with their silent constellations; there is something bigger, more permanent and important, a mystery which must be understood.

(New Forest, Hampshire)

Heart

Sallow light on old stone shifting shapes

and shadows, low light flicking across ancient faces frozen through time. Cast in candlelight as their flames gut and grow, the faces take on different dimensions, moving expressions as if stirring from sleep. It is as if the centuries are also stirring, breathing through the stillness, emphasising time's continuum.

In the Norman nave, shadows lengthen and retract, stretching and pulling across pillars, geometric patterns mimicking those of the natural world, the inceptions of icicles, spiky, angular, seen in the toothed edges of the arches, while every creak and rustle is accentuated in the silence. This wonder can only be felt in winter when the nights are as long as the shadows cast by candles or by the winter sun. In winking windows the arrangements of winter foliage foraged from the outside world stand silhouetted. Holly, ivy and yew; evergreen eternity, a hope surpassing skeletal trees.

Darkness draws us to the light, like moths to a flame, compelled by the shadow shapes dancing with the guttering candle flames, fusing with the faces which peep from the pillars. Those who carved them have long been laid to rest, sleeping silently through the centuries, their flesh consumed and bones as bare as the branches of the trees outside. Time seems intangible, yet there is meaning in mystery. This church has stood through the centuries, a beacon bearing testimony to their belief, faith and hope. And in the soft stillness I light a candle and pray. *(Wimborne, Dorset)*

Light show

Through the kaleidoscope of shifting colours come the trees; strong, stark, with limbs which seem to move; retracting and reaching out again, compelling, pulling us towards their world. Theirs is silent yet dynamic, one full of composure yet one of conversation. If only they could talk, tell us of their centuries past, for they seem to store so many memories. In this stately parkland, Lords and Ladies would have passed, perusing the pleasure of the seasons, never experiencing this magic show of colours colliding, of floodlights fusing with winter.

Feet and fingers throb beneath a cloudless sky, stars above branches emerge when the lights are lowered. We move from the modern to the ancient with the revolution of a ray of light and then the beam swings back again moving through the spectrum from violet to red and the stars are silenced. Faces form on tree trunks; gnarled ganglions or knots, expressions changing as the shadows shift from shallow to deep and back again. The trees become living, sentient beings as we enter their wintery world. Despite being in a state of torpor, they seem to see us standing there, our breath curling on the cold. We tend to anthropomorphise trees, maybe because there is something so permanent about them, or because on nights like this the excitement of a child creeps up on us.

Despite the crowds, we are shrouded in silence, the vast beyond stretching to the sky, past the sweeping shadows, the contorted fusion of faces. There is something surreal when the stars shatter in the breaking beam of light and we are left shifting through the spectrum in a bubble of brilliance, alone with the still silhouettes of trees which watch and wait before the light lowers again and the stars rejoin us. A tawny owl hoots from a distant tree, somewhere in the black, blank canvas beyond the boundaries of this light show. It adds to the suspense with its shivering cry. And so the mystery of the night takes its hold, compelling, enthralling and despite the serious cold, which has now rendered my fingers senseless, I have no desire to go indoors. *(Kingston Lacy, Dorset)*

Lavenham

Lavenham, a medieval market town, is one of the cosiest and most magical towns I know in winter. With its pot-bellied, crooked, half-timbered houses, which sway over the streets, each house seems to hold history deep in its heart, contained as secrets unless we are invited into each glowing interior. On cold, fog-filled evenings I remember the smell and curl of chimney smoke rising into a dusk-deep sky. Leaded windows seemed to glitter, catching the last glow of daylight as it melted away.

I love Lavenham at Christmastime, not just for its Christmas fayre, which provides one with an array of local crafts, food and beverages, which I always feel somehow should be recognised and cele-brated in winter, but there is also the attention which I can pay to the detail of past workmanship. Wreaths on the door-ways of old medieval houses somehow draw the eye's attention to them. The wreaths themselves display a wealth of creativity bound and interwoven with the beauties of nature. This fusion is as if we were preserving something of the bounty and fruitfulness of nature through the desolate winter months, perhaps like creating comestibles; berries are bound with evergreen or heads of hydrangea which have been dried and slicked with gold, feathers are fused with ivy and draped with ribbon. There are endless ideas and combinations, endless expressions of creativity. But it is the wooden doorframes themselves which catch my eye. Neither painted smooth or glossy, but rough, "distressed", left to their naked natural wood, many of these timeworn wonky frames are delicately carved with geometric patterns, incredibly ornate and intricate in design. I think of the skill of artisans in the past and it takes my mind back to Ely Cathedral. I am happy that some people are passionate about continuing these crafts today, that the old traditions can be carried through the centuries, that people can restore these architectural treasures. Winter is a time for reflection, and for observation. When all is exposed and the earth is laid bare, when time seems to slow down with the long dark nights and lingering mornings to give more space for contemplation, and when things are illuminated and enhanced by warm winking lights and beautiful decorations, there is no excuse not to see.

A winter's tale

There is a story behind nearly everything and on this particular night we are wondering what the story is behind the name of the pub in which we are enjoying a glass of wine and a selection of cheese with friends in front of a roaring fire. One of us scrolls down the screen of his phone, looking for the history, which he then recounts. Apparently this New Forest pub is named after a Lady Alice Lisle who lived nearby in the 17th century. She was born in 1617 and I imagine the young Alice perhaps having a beautiful but restricted upbringing in the forest. Hers would not have been the childhood of reckless freedom when forest children could go off and explore at whim, paddling in the many streams, feeding the ponies and staying out all day until it got dark. She would have been educated with the graces and accomplishments which a young lady should acquire. However, it is probable that she would have been taken out into the forest by a governess or with other family members in a horse-drawn carriage and surely her family members would have gone hunting in this forest full of deer, a forest which was created by William the Conqueror and maintained for such a purpose.

When she was 19, Alice married John Lisle, an anti-royalist politician. Whether it was a marriage of choice or of convenience, Wikipedia does not say. However, as most women of her time, Alice gave birth to multiple children (eight in total). Her husband never saw the eighth child as he fled to Switzerland after the restoration of the monarchy and was then assassinated.

Alice however, was not swayed in her nonconformist beliefs and is known to have made Moyles Court, where she resided, a refuge for displaced non-conformist ministers. Perhaps it was not only religious conviction which drove her to do this, but also a compassionate and sympathetic heart to protect those who, as had been her husband, were on the run. It was, however, to her detriment as in July 1685 she was charged with treason for harbouring John Hicks, a nonconformist preacher and member of the Duke of Monmouth's defeated army. She was tried by judge Jeffreys in Winchester and sentenced to be burnt at the stake. However, the punishment was changed to execution and in

September she spent her final night at The Eclipse Inn in Winchester, from where she stepped, through a window, to her execution the following day.

This tragic tale, although happening in the summer of 1685, makes for a chilling winter's tale. It is the type of dark narrative which one might read on cold winter's nights, for as Shakespeare says in Act 2 scene 1 of his Winter's Tale "a sad tale's best for winter". Although this tale is not about "sprites and goblins", it is all the sadder as it is true, lowering the tone of the evening for a moment as we stop and think about what it must have been like to be put to death for something so seemingly innocent and perhaps philanthropic. However, as we do not know the details, as we have only read the story from the internet, we dwell on it no longer; the pub's name having moved from being intriguing to something real and tangible. I wonder how many more stories there are out there lurking in the shadows around the names of places or things.

Outside the night is so clear and chill that it seems to permeate all clothing. We stare up at the stars. The constellation of Orion rides high above the smoky chimneys of the pub, a glowing haven against the black backdrop of trees and the wild cries of owls, for the pub is lit from the outside, its pleasingly symmetrical brick façade warm and inviting. It is itself an old building, but was maybe not around when Alice Lisle herself was. It is hard to tell its age. Orion also has a story behind him. The myth says that he was a hunter who threatened to kill all the wild animals on earth. Gaia was not pleased and so banished him to the heavens in the form of a constellation. The idea of a huntsman killing all wild animals does not sit comfortably anywhere, but especially on a winter's night in an ancient hunting forest which is one of the richest areas of wildlife in the country and is protected as a national park. (*New Forest, Hampshire*)

Metallic dusk

The sky is fast fading, an incipient inky blue slowly seeping across its blotting paper grey. And as it grows in intensity, so does the atmosphere of evening. I walk beneath birch trees, where the final fountains of leaves spill golden rustlings in the evening air and robins sing with a sparkling resonance, notes like coins sent spinning from the sky. Mars has risen golden, and Venus silver, like resplendent stars in a deepening dusk about to be engulfed in cloud. Everything seems suspended, as if waiting for night, a last call of freedom before bed, a final breath before leaves descend like golden rain and lie scattered on the path. Yet bad weather beckons with the rise of the wind; ubiquitous blackbirds start snipping at the silence, their cosy alarm calls echoing on the evening. A crow calls. Soon diurnal life will fall silent, the day having drawn its curtains. It slowly starts to rain with a gentle patter, raindrops falling softly in silver streaks. Only the robin continues to sing under the streetlights, spangling the night with its song. When it finally stops singing, all will be left to the tawny owl, which has already ventured out on the cusp of night, her distant "kerrrwik" call tweaking the twilight, a sound as mysterious as the inky sky and as thrilling as the wind which has slowly risen in the trees.

(late autumn in Dorset)

Starlight

A cold, crisp night, voluminous in its clarity as stars sprinkle the sky. Fingers throb in the sharp stillness, the billowing breath of humans and horses remind me of childhood bonfire nights. It is never that cold in November now, nor even in winter, but this winter brings a harsh cold snap and we stare up at the stars; ancient light which has travelled through time and space to reach us. And amongst the stars I see satellites slowly trailing through the darkness; twinkling as they track the sky. Man has made his mark everywhere, even in space.

Our ancestors would have seen the same stars, unravelled identical constellations. They would have experienced far more; an enriched skyscape devoid of the light pollution which now restricts our view. They would not have seen the satellites; so in this sense the skyscape has been altered and time is no longer timeless. We could not live without satellites today; so responsible are they for tracking and communication, yet the stark simplicity of winter, bringing us back to the bare bones, perhaps puts things into perspective.

Out there the satellites seem small and insignificant, creeping across the constellations which have studded the sky for centuries. Overwhelmed by the wonder of the winter night, I find the stars mind-blowing, something outside the realms of our experience and our understanding. Our ancestors would have used them for navigation, to guide their ships and to track time and season. They found stories in the stars, as a child sees pictures in patterned wallpaper. They saw Orion the hunter, and the plough, they named galaxies and individual stars after characters in myths. For it is with wonder that our imagination is released, the wonder of a child captivated by the simple things. Winter holds that wonder, and as the nights are longer than the days, it is perhaps why the winter heavens so inspire. For they inspire a sense of awe, an awe which we encounter on seeing the stars set in the infinity of space and realising that we can control very little.

Moonlight

The moon is rising; a bronze bloated sphere distorted by the earth's atmosphere. I can see its spectral light lifting the sky at the horizon long before I encounter the moon itself, yet I feel its silent presence. There is something shocking, although I have seen it put on this appearance many times before. It is quietly unnerving in its proximity, its deep bronze blush, slightly surreal as if it were a piece of modern art and had been placed out of proportion, a statement set upon the sky, a disc holding two dimensions on a flat canvas. But the contours of the clouds, the shapes and shadows reflecting the surrounding light draw more dimensions. It is as if the artist's brush went wild, sculpting a scene of the night, for this is truly a night vision, its uncanniness only lasting for a few minutes.

The path dips down between the trees. Away from the moon's steady gaze. As darkness folds in, hard, impenetrable, it is difficult to know where we are walking and where to put the next step. A tiny thread of fear begins to weave its way through me, more an uncertainty than full blown fear, a feeling of vulnerability at losing sight. We rely heavily on sight and also on light, for without light there is no sight, light which reveals everything around us, allowing us to make sense of the world. Here the world makes little sense as we stumble along holding onto each other. I realise that where the world lacks visual dimension, other senses are augmented. Trees loom as large indiscernible shapes occupying a space somewhere in front of us. Felt rather than seen, there is a sense of their mass intimating their true proximity. The river chuckles through the darkness, reassuring in its physical presence, providing us with some sense of perspective. Something cracks and I instantly and instinctively jump, simultaneously reaching for my phone. I swing the backlight around the immediate space while I fumble for the torch button. Out of the darkness glow the eyes of a cat, reflective retinas frozen, staring. I realise that I have spooked it, for it feels more comfortable under the cover of night. I flick the phone shut, turning off the torch and the darkness bounces back in, intensifying with suffocating speed until eyes grow accustomed once more.

We encounter little life here, even though it is night and we are on a country path, but it is still early, barely six o'clock. No doubt the sheep are somewhere out there, moving restlessly in the darkness, or perhaps the farmer has taken them in for the night. A fox crosses the path furtively, as if feeling exposed even under the cover of darkness. Perhaps it has sensed us, for it stops, looking over its shoulder for a brief second before dashing between the trees. I only see it because it is close and the moon is now rising, a familiar face, no longer strange or disconcerting, a welcome sight casting light into the darkness.

A few hours later I go out again, this time attracted by the light of the moon, for the landscape is bathed in brilliance; silver and silent. The shadows of the trees' bare branches form traceries across the grass like intricate lattice work. I am captivated by the stillness, the serenity of the nightscape as the moon rides majestically above, strong in its weakened state as it reflects the light of the sun. The silver wash of moonlight on a night which is barely above freezing has transformed this place into a dreamland, intangible in its perfection, ethereal. Like the moon it seems remote, lying just out of reach, and I feel like a child who wants to touch it but thinks that if they do, the spell will be broken and it will fade away, for it is like a beautiful dream from which we do not want to wake up. Yet when I walk into the "dream", the light meets me, silver flowing over my fingers, liquid light spilling over every surface. Above me the moon rides radiantly, forming a refracted halo where clumps of mackerel cloud are drifting in, catching its light. I could stay here all night, watching this wonderful wintry spectacle and the changing stage of the sky. Ensconced in silver I stare at the stars as they slip in and out from behind the clouds. I am captivated by other-worldliness, but the cold is increasing; soon my feet and fingers throb with an ache which brings me back to earth. It is too cold to stand and stare, one has to walk, and so I turn towards home where a hot water bottle will restore feet and fingers while I open the curtains to let more moonlight in.

Meteors

The winter meteor shower of the Geminids is nature's own display, providing more wonder with each starry streak. Flying from seemingly nowhere, swiftly, silently; filling minds with mystery and sparking imagination. As we crouch on the ground in a dark field, looking up so that leg and neck muscles simultaneously burn, it is worth it for the fun of seeing the blazing trail of a meteor, if only for a split second. One realises how much dark debris there is out in space, floating around in its lugubrious world until it is exposed, drawn into the atmosphere and burnt up with a brilliant flash of incandescence. It is a flame snuffed out in a second, extinguished, never to be brought back to life. Its short moment of glory is like a life in the infinite trail of time. We have such a short time to flourish before we fade, such a short time to do something worthwhile, to leave a legacy. Benefitting from the lives of generations past, we should make the most of every day, for unlike the meteor, we do not burn away; our thoughts and actions trace out eternity.

Wolf moon

Tonight a "wolf moon" has risen in the sky, the name which applies to full moons occurring in January. I imagine the wolves out in the tundra howling under a full moon, that eerie, blood-chilling call which sears the shadows of the night and reaches into every recess of the darkness. They would once have been heard here in the UK, but now they are extinct and their voices silenced.

This particular moon is also a super moon. It strides the sky, rising higher and higher with the hours, its lofty radiance illuminating shreds of cloud so that it appears remote, cold, looking on silently through a wispy veil which seems to separate it from ourselves. A lone wolf, this enigmatic moon seems more lonesome tonight as it climbs ever higher, ever more lofty and aloof.

Sometime in the early hours, it will be secretly shrouded in shadow; obliterated for a few long hours, turning a painful and curdling red, a blood moon brought about by the earth eclipsing the light of the sun. I doubt if I shall see it, even if I wake to watch it, for the forecast is thickening cloud and the dense branches of old oak trees near my window obliterate my view. I have watched eclipses in the past, the slow procedure of the moon being brought into submission, overshadowed and silenced by the earth. It will break "free" again, although still under earth's bondage, for it is never independent. As it revolves around the earth in all its haughtiness, it merely reflects the sun, is a pale imitator of it. So as I watch the wolf moon in all its loftiness, I remember that despite this being its moment of glory, it could not shine without the sun and that this is so true of us. Our moments of glory are rarely just due to ourselves.

New Year's Eve

A festive fuzz of laughter and light blends together in the town centre, ringing in ears and resounding in retinas as an overexcited crowd jostles in the jamboree. Fireworks ricochet through the night, crackling and fizzing, ripping the sky with champagne stars. The crowd gasps, silent for a few seconds. With alcohol left lingering on breath and the feeling of community spirit, the so-called tradition carries on.

Yet New Year's Eve wasn't always like this. The ancient Celts would ignite bonfires to awaken the sun. Other cultures, such as the Zoroastrian, would even jump over the leaping flames. Later in England, Churches rang their bells at midnight on New Year's Eve, a bright and jubilant welcome to the New Year. Before New Year's Eve it was also traditional to clean the house, to cleanse it of the old year and prepare it for the new. This is perhaps symbolic, for New Year is surely a time of reflection but not of regret, a time that we move forward rather than back, a time to savour sweet memories but erase the bad, a time to address the problems in the world and change them in some small way. This is perhaps where New Year's resolutions came from.

An evocative poem written in 1850 by the then Poet Laureate Alfred Lord Tennyson says everything much better than I could ever say myself. It sums up New Year for me and hearkens to the bells of the mid nineteenth century ringing out on New Year's Eve.

Ring out, wild bells (from In Memoriam)

Ring out, wild bells, to the wild sky,
The flying cloud, the frosty light:
The year is dying in the night;
Ring out, wild bells, and let him die.

Ring out the old, ring in the new,
Ring, happy bells, across the snow:
The year is going, let him go;
Ring out the false, ring in the true.

Ring out the grief that saps the mind
For those that here we see no more;
Ring out the feud of rich and poor,
Ring in redress to all mankind.

Ring out a slowly dying cause,
And ancient forms of party strife;
Ring in the nobler modes of life,
With sweeter manners, purer laws.

Ring out the want, the care, the sin,
The faithless coldness of the times;
Ring out, ring out my mournful rhymes
But ring the fuller minstrel in.

Ring out false pride in place and blood,
The civic slander and the spite;
Ring in the love of truth and right,
Ring in the common love of good.

Ring out old shapes of foul disease;
Ring out the narrowing lust of gold;
Ring out the thousand wars of old,
Ring in the thousand years of peace.

Ring in the valiant man and free,
The larger heart, the kindlier hand;
Ring out the darkness of the land,
Ring in the Christ that is to be.

I cannot imagine the cold and the heart-
ache for those who feel cast out into the
winter without home or shelter and my
hope is that some of the proceeds from this
book will help in some small way for those
people to come in from the cold.